Carr has clearly taken a great deal of time, effort and prayerful thought to assemble this devotional. There are a multitude of God-given insights to be had, many of which I've never before considered. Definitely worth reading and praying about.

—Frank King,
Christian blogger at FranksCottage.blog

There are many different approaches to creating resources for your devotional and quiet times. Philip Edward Carr takes a unique approach by beginning with looking at the 3:16 verses throughout the Bible and then looking in depth at the gospel of John where we find the most famous 3:16 verse in Scripture.

Carr's approach is one where he invites you unapologetically to discover more and more truths about what God is calling us to become as people who follow the way of Jesus. As a reader, you will develop Biblical understanding and literacy as you journey through this simple yet profound devotional book. By declaring a key message in each day's devotional, readers are able to quickly understand some foundational, yet deep Biblical themes found throughout the entire Biblical narrative that Phil walks his readers through.

In Scripture, it says that "Scripture will not return void" (Isaiah 55:11) and this devotional certainly will illuminate for you how personal, yet powerful Scripture truly is. After reading this devotional, I am passionate about memorizing the 3:16 verses found throughout the pages of God's story – the Bible.

Carr's personal anecdotes and reflections invite you to share your own desires and passions to understand God in a way that you most definitely will be changed.

—Matt Wilks,
Author of *Cultivate*, Canadian Youth Worker,
Regional Minister for Alberta Baptist Association

THE 3:16 VERSES OF THE BIBLE
and Devotional Readings from the Gospel of John

PHILIP EDWARD CARR

THE 3:16 VERSES OF THE BIBLE
Copyright © 2022 by Phillip Edward Carr

Author photo by Calgary Custom Photo Services

All rights reserved. Neither this publication nor any part of this publication may be reproduced or transmitted in any form or by any means, electronic or mechanical, including photocopying, recording or any information storage and retrieval system, without permission in writing from the author.

Unless otherwise indicated, all scripture quotations are from the King James Version of the Bible, which is in the public domain. • Scripture quotations marked (NKJV) are taken from the New King James Version®. Copyright © 1982 by Thomas Nelson, Inc. Used by permission. All rights reserved. • Scripture quotations marked (ESV) are taken from The Holy Bible, English Standard Version® (ESV®), copyright © 2001 by Crossway, a publishing ministry of Good News Publishers. Used by permission. All rights reserved. • Scripture quotations marked (GNT) are taken from the Good News Translation® (Today's English Version, Second Edition), Copyright © 1992 American Bible Society. All rights reserved. Bible text from the Good News Translation (GNT) is not to be reproduced in copies or otherwise by any means except as permitted in writing by American Bible Society, 1865 Broadway, New York, NY 10023. • Scripture quotations marked (HCSB) are taken from the Holman Christian Standard Bible®, Used by Permission HCSB ©1999,2000,2002,2003,2009 Holman Bible Publishers. Holman Christian Standard Bible®, Holman CSB®, and HCSB® are federally registered trademarks of Holman Bible Publishers. • Scripture quotations marked (RSV) are taken from the Revised Standard Version of the Bible, copyright © 1946, 1952, and 1971 the Division of Christian Education of the National Council of the Churches of Christ in the United States of America. Used by permission. All rights reserved. • Scripture quotations marked (NCV) are taken from the New Century Version®. Copyright © 2005 by Thomas Nelson. Used by permission. All rights reserved.

ISBN: 978-1-4866-2345-7
eBook ISBN: 978-1-4866-2346-4

Printed in Canada

Word Alive Press
119 De Baets Street Winnipeg, MB R2J 3R9
www.wordalivepress.ca

Cataloguing in Publication information can be obtained from Library and Archives Canada.

With thanks to Linda for her support,
and deep appreciation to everyone who encouraged me to keep writing
(especially Carolyn Arends).

To Robert:
Thank you for
This!) your story!

CONTENTS

INTRODUCTION ix

PART ONE
THE 3:16 VERSES 1

PART TWO
DEVOTIONS FROM THE GOSPEL OF JOHN 137

CONCLUSION 191

ABOUT THE AUTHOR 193

INTRODUCTION

THIS IS A DAILY devotional that you can read in three months. It consists of two parts. The first section is a journey through the "3:16" verses of the Bible. The second section is a journey through the Gospel of John. In the first part, we take a book-by-book trip through the Bible and see the unique aspects of each one. In the second part, I show how Jesus proclaimed Himself to be the Messiah and how His actions bore out His claims. Even the opponents of Jesus understood that this was His message.

PART ONE: THE 3:16 VERSES

The idea for this section came to me when I read 1 Timothy 3:16. Most Christians know John 3:16 by heart, and I started to wonder what other "3:16 verses" might hold. I then started that journey through the Bible. There are seventeen books in the Bible that do not have a 3:16 verse. In those cases, I have written about a different verse to ensure that each book of the Bible is represented. In the Old Testament, there are nine books for which I've written about a different verse in chapter three—usually the last verse of that chapter. In Obadiah and Haggai, I write about verse sixteen from an earlier chapter. In the New Testament, six books don't have a 3:16 passage. In three cases, I discuss verse sixteen from a different chapter, and in three others I write about another verse (Titus 3:15: 2 John 1:13; 3 John 1:14). In some cases, I've included one or two surrounding verses to put the selected verse in context.

PART TWO: THE GOSPEL OF JOHN

I like John's Gospel because he gives a clear response to those who say that Jesus did not see Himself as the Messiah, and those who claim that He was merely a good, pacifist teacher of the day. We will take a chapter-by-chapter journey through John. On occasion, I have split the chapter into two parts.

SUMMARY

Both parts of this book follow a daily format. First the subject verse is quoted, and then I share the key message from that chapter or book. I then discuss the verse and its significance. I end with an application for the reader for today. I have headed each section with a day (i.e., "Day One") rather than having chapters.

The first part of the book could be described as a "tea sampler" of the Bible. I trust that you will gain an introduction to the books of the Bible and then decide if a particular book, or books, speaks to your situation and if you'd like to read more from that book. You will also gain an appreciation for the fact that *"all scripture is given by inspiration of God"* (which is from a 3:16 verse!) In the second part of the book, you can walk with John and experience the unique insights from *"the disciple whom Jesus loved."* I hope that this book will contribute to your biblical knowledge and literacy in an easy-to-read devotional format.

PART ONE
THE 3:16 VERSES

1

GENESIS 3:16

Then God said to the woman, "I will cause you to have much trouble when you are pregnant, and when you give birth to children, you will have great pain. You will greatly desire your husband, but he will rule over you." (NCV)

KEY MESSAGE:
SIN HAS CONSEQUENCES

I WAS IN ATTENDANCE when each of our three children was born, despite my protests that having me faint wasn't likely to add anything to the process. During pre-natal classes, the instructor would occasionally remind the men that we needed to pay attention or we might not be allowed in the labour and delivery room. I replied that I didn't see any threat in that possibility. I'm glad that I wasn't required to be an active participant in the birthing process! The delivery of our oldest son was complicated enough that the attending physician had to call in a specialist for assistance. In hindsight, it was probably a blessing that this happened with our first child, because I didn't know enough to be worried that this was a potential problem. Happily for us, all three of our children are alive and healthy.

While this verse focuses on the consequences of sin for the woman, Eve, a reading of the entire chapter shows that no one is exempt from sin's stain and its consequences. God tells Adam (v. 17) that the ground will be *"cursed ... for thy sake."* He will now have to work very hard for his food and battle thorns and thistles to produce a crop. Even the serpent bears the consequences of sin, being *"cursed above all cattle"* (v. 14). Verse fifteen speaks of enmity between the woman and the serpent, which is no doubt the source of the ongoing battle between the woman and the snake in the comic strip *B.C.*

Sin forced humanity to leave the Garden of Eden. Despite Joni Mitchell's wistful lyrics in the song "Woodstock," we can't go back to the garden. Moreover, the way to set your soul free isn't by camping out on the land or attending hedonistic music festivals. The only way to be free from sin is by trusting in the righteousness of the second Adam, Jesus Christ, and His offer of salvation through His death and resurrection.

APPLICATION FOR TODAY:

What sin is causing consequences for you today? Do you need to confess to God and seek forgiveness?

EXODUS 3:16

Go and gather the older leaders and tell them this: "The Lord, the God of your ancestors Abraham, Isaac, and Jacob, has appeared to me. He said, I care about you, and I have seen what has happened to you in Egypt." (NCV)

KEY MESSAGE:
GOD EQUIPS THE CALLED; HE DOESN'T JUST CALL THE EQUIPPED.

EXODUS 3 DESCRIBES THE encounter Moses had at the burning bush. The first application for us could be that when God is going to ask you to do something, He'll get your attention and wait for you to respond. While lying awake in my bed one night, I was having a prayer time with God. I asked Him why He seemed to wait until 3:00 a.m. to speak with me. He replied, "Because this is the only time when I can get your attention." We need open eyes and ears to make sure that we don't miss God's call to us.

Much of this chapter consists of a dialogue between God and Moses, with Moses raising objections to God's call and plan. In verses thirteen and fourteen, Moses asks God what he's supposed to say when the children of Israel ask him for God's name. This leads to the memorable reply in verse fourteen: *"And God said unto Moses, I AM THAT I AM: and he said, Thus shalt thou say to the children of Israel, I AM hath sent me unto you."*

The balance of Exodus 3, and much of the next chapter, continues the exchange between God and Moses, with Moses continuing to raise objections, and God—albeit with what appears to be some irritation—answering them. Finally, Moses obeys God's call, and Exodus 4 ends on a hopeful note: *"And the people believed: and when they had heard that the Lord had visited the children of Israel, and that he had looked upon their affliction, they bowed their heads and worshipped"* (v. 31). As we know, it wasn't all smooth sailing after this, but in the end, as always, God prevailed.

We don't always expect God's call to us. Moses didn't anticipate God's call and certainly wasn't seeking it. The important thing is to answer the call when it comes, even if we're surprised by it. Some years ago, we had a children's choir in our church. It had always been my firm belief that my ministry did not include working with children. Yet one Sunday morning as I sat in the service, I distinctly heard God tell me: "You need to offer to help Shawn with the choir." Similar to Moses, my reaction was, "I assume you're speaking to someone in the row behind me, God, because that message can't be intended for me!" But the following Sunday, the call came again, and I finally obeyed and asked Shawn if I could help in some fashion. That led to a very rewarding (at least for me) time of attending the rehearsals and bringing a devotion to the children each week. I enjoyed the experience immensely.

APPLICATION FOR TODAY:

If you hear God's call, answer it and see what God has in store for you!

LEVITICUS 3:16

The priest will burn these parts on the altar as food. It is an offering made by fire, and its smell is pleasing to the Lord. All the fat belongs to the Lord.

(NCV)

KEY MESSAGE:
GOD IS PLEASED WITH OUR SINCERE WORSHIP.

THROUGHOUT SCRIPTURE, PEOPLE MAKE offerings and sacrifices to God. Obviously, God doesn't need our offerings or sacrifices, since everything already belongs to Him. But God is pleased with our obedience and acts of service. Scripture contains both good and bad examples of sacrifices, starting with the offerings made by Cain and Abel. God tells Cain that if he does well, he will be accepted, but if not, "*sin lieth at the door*" (Genesis 4:7).

There are lessons for us from both the Old and New Testaments. First, don't go "off the page" with your own idea of how to worship God. Nadab and Abihu try this in the Old Testament, and God strikes them dead, even though they're priests and the sons of Aaron. Later on, the children of Israel decide that they can transport the ark of the covenant by ox cart, even though God had expressly decreed that it was only to be carried on poles supported on the shoulders of the priests. This decision costs another man his life when he touches the ark because the oxen had stumbled.

In the New Testament, Jesus approves the humble offering made by a poor widow over the larger, ostentatious offerings of the wealthy. God has high standards, but they're not unattainable for anyone. Approach God with reverence and a sincere heart. Don't ignore any clear instructions from God along the way. Take the time and effort needed to spend proper quality time with God.

APPLICATION FOR TODAY:

Consider how you are worshipping God and what sacrifice you might need to make to be pleasing to the Lord.

NUMBERS 3:16

And Moses numbered them according to the word of the Lord, as he was commanded.

KEY MESSAGE:
FAITHFUL OBEDIENCE TO GOD'S COMMANDS IS IMPORTANT.

GOD TOLD MOSES TO take a full census of all the people of Israel. On this occasion, God told him to include the Levites, who fulfilled the priestly role. God wanted Moses to know the full extent of the population of Israel. Later on, however, David decided to take a census of the people on his own initiative. God didn't direct this census, and it appears to have been motivated by pride on David's part—a desire to know how many people the Lord had placed under his leadership. This census was sinful, and God brought judgment upon the people.

David's commander-in-chief, Joab, advised David against conducting this census! Joab often acted on his own and did what he considered expedient, but on this occasion, he was correct. In 2 Samuel 24:3, Joab replies to David: *"Now the Lord thy God add unto the people, how many soever they be, a hundred-fold, and that thy eyes of my lord may see it; but why doth my lord the king delight in this thing?"* Verse four then tells us that *"the king's word prevailed against Joab and against the captains of the host."* In the parallel passage in 1 Chronicles 21:6, we're told that David's directive was so repugnant to Joab that Joab refused to number the Levites or the Benjamites. Before we reach the end of 2 Samuel 24, the prophet Gad approaches David and informs him that the Lord has judged David's sin, and that David can choose his punishment from a list of three options: seven years of famine, three months of fleeing before his enemies, or three days of pestilence in the land. As a result of David's rash command, seventy thousand men perished (2 Samuel 24:15)! Sin has consequences that might extend far beyond ourselves.

APPLICATION FOR TODAY:

Consider if there is any area of your life where you have gone off the page of God's directions. If so, repent and ask for His forgiveness and direction.

DEUTERONOMY 3:16

And unto the Reubenites and unto the Gadites I gave from Gilead even unto the river Arnan half the valley, and the border even unto the river Jabbok, which is the border of the children of Ammon.

KEY MESSAGE:
GOD ALLOCATED THE LAND OF ISRAEL TO HIS PEOPLE.

THIS VERSE, AND THIS section of the Old Testament, are vitally important today because many continue to debate the entitlement of the Jewish people to this land. The Bible is very clear that God allocated the land to His chosen people, and it states where the borders are located. There can be no debate on this point. Those who rage against Israel, whether they admit it or not, are raging against God. In some cases, their eyes are blinded to the truth. They're actually motivated by a demonic hatred of the Jewish people, a wilful refusal to accept that the Bible is true, or both. Many today want to use the word "Palestine" to describe this land. It's significant that this word only appears once in the entire King James Version of the Bible (Joel 3:4).

It's a tragic reality of history that the Jewish people suffered for so many years without an official homeland until Israel was established in 1948, but that doesn't invalidate their rightful claim to this part of the world. God clearly allocated the lands to them, and many maps found in various editions of the Bible can show you the extent of their lands. Given that God Himself made these allocations, there is no sound argument that people can advance against them.

APPLICATION FOR TODAY:
God has allocated the land of Israel to His chosen people, the Jewish nation. There is no valid argument to be made against Israel's right to exist as a nation.

JOSHUA 3:16

That the waters which came down from above stood and rose up upon a heap very far from the city Adam, that is beside Zaretan: and those that came down toward the sea of the plain, even the salt sea, failed, and were cut off: and the people passed over right against Jericho.

KEY MESSAGE:
SOMETIMES GOD "PASSES OVER."
SOMETIMES HIS PEOPLE GET TO "PASS OVER."

IN THIS CHAPTER, GOD provides a miraculous way for His people to cross the Jordan River: He stops it for them and creates a land bridge. This is one time when the children of Israel were truly faithful and trusted God to provide for them. It was also one of the early challenges for Joshua in his time of leadership.

At the end of the previous book (Deuteronomy), Moses died. Now Joshua is the leader. Joshua 1 records his opening address to the people. In verse seventeen, the people assure Joshua that they will obey him, "*as we hearkened unto Moses in all things.*" I've often wondered whether Joshua cringed or rejoiced when he heard those words! Did the people actually believe that they had hearkened to Moses in all things? If so, they must have had very short memories.

Nonetheless, in Joshua 3:5, Joshua says this to the people: "*Sanctify yourselves: for tomorrow the Lord will do wonders among you.*" It's not clear whether Joshua knew specifically what wonders the Lord was going to do or merely spoke in faith, knowing that God would act to help His children. What happened the next day is beautifully summarized in the song "Beyond Belief" by Petra. The children of Israel were to follow the priests who were carrying the ark of the covenant. The writer of Joshua informs us (v. 15) that the Jordan River overflows its banks at the time of harvest. This means that the priests were able to walk into the water at the same level as the banks beside the river—and then God stopped the river and provided the dry land for them to continue. This is significant: if the priests had merely stopped at the edge of the river and expected God to part the waters first, He would not have done so. He wanted to see faithful action on their part. The priests were faithful, which takes us to this verse: the waters parted, and the people went on their way! Joshua then had the people select one man from each of the twelve tribes to take a stone from the dry river bed to make a memorial of their crossing. Once this had been accomplished and all the people had crossed the Jordan River, the waters returned to their place. Joshua puts this epilogue on the events: *"That all the people of the earth might know the hand of the Lord, that it is mighty: that ye might fear the Lord your God forever"* (Joshua 4:24).

APPLICATION FOR TODAY:

Waters never part until our feet get wet! If God is calling you to action, move forward and be faithful!

JUDGES 3:16

But Ehud made him a dagger which had two edges, of a cubit length; and he hid it under his raiment upon his right thigh.

KEY MESSAGE:
GOD SENDS JUDGMENT UPON THE WICKED, AND THE RESULTS ARE NOT ALWAYS PRETTY.

IN THIS CHAPTER, EHUD kills the King of Moab. To set the stage: The book of Judges follows a regrettable but familiar pattern. The people get delivered from oppression. The people rebel against God. God delivers the people into oppression to draw them back to Him. The people eventually cry out to God. God delivers the people from oppression—and they drift away from Him again until the next period of oppression.

This chapter begins with the people doing evil and serving false gods. The Lord delivers them into the hands of the Mesopotamians for eight years until they cry out to Him and He delivers them. After forty years, they again drift away from God, and He delivers them into the hand of Eglon, the King of Moab, for eighteen years. God then raises up Ehud, from the tribe of Benjamin, to deliver them.

The choice of Ehud shows that God is able to use anyone willing to be God's servant. Ehud was from the tribe of Benjamin, which was the smallest tribe in Israel. He was left-handed, which was not viewed favourably at that time. (The Latin word "sinister" means "left-handed.") But in this passage, we see how God uses that. Being left-handed, Ehud hides the dagger on his right thigh. In his private audience with King Eglon, he is able to retrieve the dagger with his left hand and thrust it into his victim. Verse twenty-two contains the rather gory details that the entire dagger, including the handle, disappear into the king's fat belly, so Ehud can't even retrieve his weapon! Emboldened by Ehud's actions, Israel rises up against Moab and subdues that nation. Verse thirty tells us that the land then was at rest for eighty years.

Now, I'm not recommending that we all start making daggers and attacking our enemies, but I am recommending that none of us make an excuse as to why God cannot use us in our circumstances. In this case, Ehud was a very unlikely candidate to deliver Israel, and there was a definite element of risk in his actions. But he had the courage to move forward and trust God for the result.

APPLICATION FOR TODAY:

God is able to use anyone who is willing to be used by Him.

RUTH 3:16

She went to her mother-in-law, Naomi, who asked her: "How did it go, my daughter?" Then Ruth told her everything the man had done for her.
(HCSB)

KEY MESSAGE:
GOD PROTECTS HIS PEOPLE IN WAYS WE WOULD NEVER EXPECT OR PLAN.

THERE ARE MANY POWERFUL spiritual lessons in this book. We can certainly see faithfulness in the lives of the main characters: Boaz, Naomi, and Ruth. It's also been noted that Ruth was not of the house of Israel. She was a Moabite, yet God chose her to be the mother of Obed, who was the grandfather of David. Ruth meant what she said when she told Naomi that *"thy people shall be my people, and thy God my God"* (1:16).

This verse comes after Ruth had been gleaning (picking up leftover grain) in the field of Boaz. Boaz clearly had a heart of compassion. When he learned Ruth's history (from one of his servants), he tipped the deck in her favour by telling the reapers to deliberately leave more grain for her to find.

Chapter three contains one of the most unusual courtship stories in the Bible! Naomi instructs Ruth to go to the threshing floor and lie down at the feet of Boaz after he lies down to sleep for the night. Boaz then meticulously follows the customs of the day. He confirms that he is a kinsman of Naomi—and thus of Ruth, given the death of her husband—but that there is one kinsman who is closer in line to Ruth and thus has the first opportunity (or obligation) to marry her. Boaz then presents the opportunity to that kinsman, but he declines the opportunity to marry Ruth lest he *"mar his own inheritance"* (4:6), since the firstborn son would be seen as the son of Ruth and her prior husband, now deceased. While this all seems very odd to us today, God had a plan for the line of the Messiah, and this piece of the puzzle fit perfectly into the hole designed for it!

APPLICATION FOR TODAY:

God moves in the hearts of His people, so it's important for us to pay attention to and obey His prompting.

I SAMUEL 3:16

*Then Eli called Samuel, and said
Samuel, my son. And he answered,
Here am I.*

KEY MESSAGE:
GOD CALLS US IN UNIQUE WAYS.

THE BIRTH OF SAMUEL came about after the desperate prayers of his mother, Hannah, to have a son, and a somewhat offhand comment by Eli the priest. Observing Hannah praying in the temple, Eli initially thought she was drunk (apparently because her lips were moving but she was praying in silence). Upon being corrected by Hannah, and hearing that she was crying out to God out of grief and pain, Eli changed his critique into this blessing in 1 Samuel 1:17: *"… Go in peace: and the God of Israel grant thee thy petition that thou hast asked of him."* God indeed was faithful, as the previously barren Hannah gave birth to Samuel. True to her word, she dedicated her son to the Lord, and the boy went on to serve Eli at the temple.

Chapter three relates how the Lord called Samuel. The writer reminds us in verse one that *"the word of the LORD was precious in those days; there was no open vision."* As a result, when Samuel first heard a voice calling him, he assumed that the voice belonged to Eli, and he ran to see what the priest needed. It even took Eli a period of time to realize that it must be the Lord who was calling Samuel, and then Eli instructed Samuel how to answer.

In verses eleven through fourteen, The Lord speaks to Samuel and informs him that He will judge the house of Eli because his sons have not been faithful in fulfilling their priestly duties. Instead, they have preyed upon the people. That takes us to verse sixteen. One morning, Eli calls Samuel to him and wants to know what the Lord has said to Samuel. Eli even goes so far as to say that

Samuel shouldn't hide anything from him. Samuel then informs Eli of all that the Lord has said, even though it's a message of judgment upon Eli and his household. Eli's response seems to hold a note of sad resignation: "*It is the Lord: let him do what seemeth him good.*" One wonders whether a sincere effort at repentance would have changed the result, but it appears as though Eli's sons were not the type to be persuaded to change their ways.

Samuel went on to be one of the leading figures in Israel, while Eli and his two sons died on the same day—the infamous day when the Philistines captured the ark of the covenant (1 Samuel 4:17–18). God also remembered the faithfulness of Hannah, for 1 Samuel 2:21 informs us that Hannah and her husband, Elkanah, were blessed with three sons and two daughters.

APPLICATION FOR TODAY:

When God calls you, be ready to respond. His voice is usually the quiet one.

2 SAMUEL 3:16

And her husband went with her along weeping behind her to Bahurim. Then said Abner unto him, Go, return. And he returned.

KEY MESSAGE:
IN THE OLD TESTAMENT, KINGS DID WHAT THEY NEEDED TO DO IN ORDER TO SHOW THEIR POWER.

HAVE YOU EVER RE-GIFTED something? This is the practice of rewrapping a gift you didn't like or couldn't use and then giving it to someone else. King Saul might set the standard for re-gifting, because he managed to re-gift his daughter, Michal. David was in love with Michal. When Saul heard this, he tried to make the situation work to his advantage. He let David know that the dowry for David to marry Michal would be the foreskins of one hundred Philistines. In Saul's mind, this was a win-win for him. Either David would dispose of a large number of his enemies, or David would be killed and cease to be a potential threat to his kingdom. David fulfilled the task and married Michal. Later on, when Saul's rage against David increased, Michal helped her husband escape. Saul then re-gifted Michal by giving her to another man, Phaltiel, the son of Laish.

Second Samuel 3:16 is set in the context of David establishing his kingdom and asserting control. Abner, who had been Saul's righthand man, was now trying to curry favour with David. In verse twelve of this chapter, Abner seeks to form an alliance with David. In reply, David set this condition: *"Thou shalt not see my face, except thou first bring Michal Saul's daughter, when thou comest to see my face"* (v. 13). In response, Abner has Michal taken from her husband

and returned to David. Predictably, Phaltiel goes with her, weeping, until Abner tells him to return or face the consequences—presumably death.

It's hard not to sympathize with Phaltiel. He had done nothing wrong, and it's not clear how Michal felt about all of this. We know that she loved David and wanted to marry him initially. Later on, however, she was somewhat critical of her husband when he danced before the Lord as the ark of the covenant came back to its rightful place. We can't glean too much information from the Bible, since the only two verses that discuss this incident are 1 Samuel 25:44 (which tells us about Saul re-gifting his daughter) and this verse. It's not even clear if David is motivated by love or merely the need to assert his control and make the statement that "Michal is mine because I paid for her."

APPLICATION FOR TODAY:

Not all Scripture verses are easy to understand in today's society, but they can cause us to think. In this case, perhaps one lesson would be for us to examine the relationships we have with others to ensure that our motives are pure!

1 KINGS 3:16

Then came there two women, that were harlots, unto the king, and stood before him.

KEY MESSAGE:
KING SOLOMON STARTS TO SHOW HIS WISDOM.

YOU PROBABLY KNOW THIS story. Early in his reign, King Solomon heard from God. The Lord asked Solomon what gift he would like to receive, and Solomon asked for wisdom to govern well. God granted this request. The very next day, Solomon had the opportunity to put his wisdom to the test.

Two women came before the king to ask him to solve their dispute. Each of them had given birth to a child. During the night, one of the children had died. The question was, which child had died. One mother said that the other woman had taken her child in the night and replaced him with her deceased child. The other woman told the same tale. King Solomon's response: bring me a sword and cut the child in two; each of them can have half of the child. The brilliance in his solution was that the true mother of the living child couldn't bear to see her son killed, so she said that the living child should be given to the other woman. For her part, the other woman was content to have the child cut in two. Solomon then knew which mother had the living child and rescinded his original command, directing that the child be given to the mother who did not want to see the boy killed.

Again, it's hard to fit this story into our context, particularly in a society that sees nothing wrong with women choosing to murder their children through abortion. One also assumes that Solomon had insight as to which woman was the real mother of the child and that this test was for the benefit of those in attendance so that he could show his wisdom to his new subjects. One can't imagine that he would have allowed the child to be cut in half, and we must be thankful that the servant bringing the sword was slow on the execution (literally).

Another message for us is to treat all people equally and with respect. The Bible tells us that the two women were harlots, yet King Solomon didn't turn them away or ask why he should even bother to hear their complaint. It behooves us to treat all of God's children with respect and the knowledge that God loves them.

APPLICATION FOR TODAY:

Do not be afraid to ask God for wisdom. Be willing to share that insight with all people.

12

2 KINGS 3:16

And he [Elisha] said: Thus says the LORD: Make this valley full of ditches.

KEY MESSAGE:
GOD'S POWER IS NEVER LIMITED BY CIRCUMSTANCES.

THREE SEPARATE KINGS HAD assembled to try to quell a rebellion started by the King of Moab. The three kings in the alliance were Joram, King of Israel (the son of Ahab); Jehoshaphat, the King of Judah; and the King of Edom (who is not identified by name in this passage). The allied kings had exhausted their water supply, and Joram was ready to abandon hope. In 2 Kings 3:10b, he laments that "*… the Lord hath called these three kings together, to deliver them into the hand of Moab!*" It was Jehoshaphat, King of Judah, who had asked if there was a prophet of Yahweh whom they might consult. One of Joram's servants suggested that they call Elisha.

Elisha wasn't intimidated by earthly authority. He told the three kings that if the King of Judah hadn't been among them, he wouldn't even deign to speak with the other two men. At verse sixteen, Elisha tells them that they need to dig ditches to hold the water that the Lord would send to them. Elisha informs the kings that even though they wouldn't see any wind or feel any rain, God would fill the ditches with water. He reminds them (v. 18) that this is an easy thing for God to accomplish.

Not only did the water arrive, but it fooled the Moabites and played a key role in their downfall. When they saw the sunlight reflecting off the water in the ditches, they believed that it was blood and that the three kings had turned against one another. The Moabites thought that they would have an easy time looting the remaining spoils—but instead, they became the spoils for the allied kings.

APPLICATION FOR TODAY:
Trust God and don't be intimidated by your circumstances.

13

1 CHRONICLES 3:16
And the sons of Jehoiakim: Jeconiah his son, Zedekiah his son.

KEY MESSAGE:
THERE ARE NO UNIMPORTANT VERSES IN THE BIBLE.

THE BOOKS OF 1 and 2 Chronicles often don't come across as very riveting to us. However, we know that God has a reason for every verse in the Bible. In his commentary on the Bible, Matthew Henry noted that: "All scripture is profitable, though not all alike profitable ..."[1]

I heard another speaker who put these verses in a different light. He said that when we get to heaven and meet someone such as Jeconiah, we wouldn't want to say, "I've never heard of that name before," only to have him reply, "My name's mentioned in the Bible. Did you read the Bible?" I must confess that while I have read the Bible more than thirty times, I wouldn't pretend to say I recall every single name in the book.

The genealogies in these books were very important to the children of Israel because they established which people belonged to a particular tribe, and different tribes had different roles. The sons of Levi, for example, were the priestly tribe. In the book of Genesis, Israel spoke a specific blessing over each of his sons, and those words were the legacy of each tribe. Words of blessing are important. In the time of Nehemiah, the genealogies showed who could be counted as true children of Israel and thus welcome to worship the true God.

Second Chronicles 3 contains a list of the sons of David. This is a very important chapter, because we know that Jesus was to be born from the

---

[1] Matthew Henry, *Matthew Henry's Commentary on the Whole Bible, Vol. 2* (McLean, VA: MacDonald Publishing Company, 1980), 837.

lineage of David. Sure enough, the Jeconiah mentioned in this verse appears in the lineage of Jesus as recorded in Matthew 1:11.

APPLICATION FOR TODAY:
We can rely on the Bible as being historically accurate and trustworthy.

14

2 CHRONICLES 3:16

And he made chains, as in the oracle, and put them on the heads of pillars; and made an hundred pomegranates, and put them on chains.

KEY MESSAGE:
GOD CARES ABOUT OUR ATTITUDE AND APPROACH TO WORSHIP.

THIS VERSE IS PART of a very long section of the Bible that describes the construction of the temple. Second Chronicles 2:1 begins: *"And Solomon determined to build a house for the name of the Lord, and an house for his kingdom."* The balance of chapter two is largely spent detailing the preparations, such as assembling the materials needed. This included securing a supply of lumber from Huram (some translations say Hiram), the King of Tyre. In verses eleven and twelve, Huram speaks in glowing terms about Solomon as king.

Chapter three opens with the start of construction of the temple. The subject verse for today is part of a description of the decorations inside the temple. Chapter four continues the narrative, opening with a description of the altar of brass and the twelve oxen who supported the *"molten sea"* (v. 2). Chapter five tells us that *"all the work that Solomon made for the house of the Lord was finished"* (v. 1). It was time to celebrate the accomplishment with a feast and a worship service! Chapter six records Solomon's speech and a great prayer to the Lord at the worship service. Chapter seven informs us that when Solomon had finished his prayer, the Lord honoured the occasion as *"fire came down from heaven, and consumed the burnt offering and the sacrifices; and the glory of the Lord filled the house"* (v. 1).

This great temple no longer stands. In Jesus' day, many of the people were proud of the temple. To them, the building represented God and His blessing upon Israel. While buildings can be impressive and helpful for worship, we need to recall the words of Jesus that *"the kingdom of God is within you"* (Luke 17:21b). We need to consider our attitude and our approach as we enter into worship. Are we there to honour God, or to seek our own enjoyment or edification? Have we prepared our hearts to honour God? As much as we might wish we had been present for Solomon's worship service, it's good to recall that the preparations for worship occupy approximately five chapters of the Bible!

APPLICATION FOR TODAY:

Prepare your heart before you enter into worship of God. Understand His holiness.

15

EZRA 3:13

EZRA IS THE FIRST book in the Bible (but not the last) where I can't discuss a "3:16 verse" because the verse doesn't exist. Chapter three of Ezra ends at verse thirteen. Here is that verse:

> So that the people could not discern the noise of the shout of joy from the noise of the weeping of the people: for the people shouted with a loud shout, and the noise was heard afar off.

KEY MESSAGE:
WE OFTEN NEED A TIME OF RESTORATION IN WHICH WE RETURN TO THE LORD.

Ezra is a book about the rebuilding of the temple. After a period of exile in Persia, Cyrus the king issued a remarkable decree: he acknowledged that the Lord God of heaven had given him his power, and he honoured God by allowing those members of the Jewish people who wished to leave Persia to return to Jerusalem to rebuild and restore the temple.

Ezra 3 recounts the start of these efforts. The temple had been destroyed to such an extent that the builders had to start with the foundation. Chapter three recounts the worship service when the laying of the foundation was completed, and the subject verse encapsulates the overwhelming conflicting emotions people can feel at one time. Those who remembered the original temple wept as they thought of its destruction, the anguish, the exile they had gone through, and the effort needed to get to this point. Those who hadn't lived through the earlier destruction were more celebratory, for they saw only the accomplishment of making a new temple for the Lord. As verse thirteen tells us, it was hard to distinguish the sound of weeping from the shouts of joy, and the combined noise could be heard "*afar off.*" Do we worship with such exuberance today?

Many commentators have also noted that God called Cyrus by name before Cyrus was even born. Nothing is beyond the knowledge and reach of God! Our God called and appointed Cyrus before he was born and decreed that a pagan king would acknowledge Yahweh and issue the order to allow the Jewish people to return and rebuild the temple.

APPLICATION FOR TODAY:

God's power is unlimited. Our part is to worship, obey, and act in accordance with His direction.

16

NEHEMIAH 3:16

After him repaired Nehemiah the son of Azbak, the ruler of the half part of Bethzur, unto the place against the sepulchers of David, and to the pool that was made, and unto the house of the mighty.

KEY MESSAGE:
NOTHING IS IMPOSSIBLE IF GOD IS IN CHARGE OF THE PROJECT.

THE BOOK OF NEHEMIAH is about restoration and renewal. While the rebuilding of the walls of Jerusalem is the most obvious physical evidence of restoration, Nehemiah also had to restore in the people a desire to repent and serve God properly once again.

Nehemiah was one of the exiles and served King Artaxerxes as his cupbearer. He received word from his brother, Hanani, that the walls of Jerusalem had been destroyed and its gates had been burned (1:3). This news caused Nehemiah great distress, so much so that the king noticed the change in Nehemiah's attitude. God moved in the heart of the king, as can be seen in his discussion with Nehemiah in chapter two. The king asked Nehemiah about the reason for his sad appearance, listened to his concerns, and granted Nehemiah's request to be allowed to return to Jerusalem to rebuild its walls.

Upon arriving in Jerusalem, Nehemiah took time to assess the extent of the problem. Chapter two records how he left the city at night to conduct his assessment before rallying the people to rise to the task of rebuilding the wall. It also acquaints us with the three main opponents of this project: Sanballat, Tobiah, and Geshem.

Chapter three opens with the start of the work of rebuilding the wall around Jerusalem. We're told the names of the people who took charge of each section of the wall and the work they performed. Our subject verse comes halfway through chapter three and is a good example of how each verse is laid out, with the names of the workers and the area where they were working.

Chapter four sets out how the opposition to the project intensified, to the point that the workers had a trowel in one hand and a sword in the other. The balance of the book is a good study of restoration and the opposition Nehemiah faced. He didn't just oversee the construction of the wall; he also restored the observance of the Sabbath (13:15–22) and chastised those who had married foreign wives (13:23–27). Throughout this book, the dedication and focus of Nehemiah are clear. He was completely dedicated to God, and nothing was going to deter him from his mission. Along the way, he enlisted a solid team of people who were obviously willing to do the work but just needed someone to lead them. He also rebuffed the persistent opposition from his foes. Throughout all of this, he sought God's face in prayer and relied upon God's faithful support.

APPLICATION FOR TODAY:

When you have your assignment from God, rally your team and don't be deterred by opposition.

17

ESTHER 3:15

IN THE BOOK OF Esther, chapter three ends with verse fifteen, which reads as follows:

> The posts went out, being hastened by the king's commandment, and the decree was given in Shushan the palace. And the king and Haman sat down to drink; but the city Shushan was perplexed.

KEY MESSAGE:
VISCERAL HATRED OF THE JEWISH PEOPLE IS NOT NEW, BUT GOD PROTECTS HIS CHILDREN.

For most commentators, the book of Esther is an example of how God worked to prevent the extinction of His chosen people, the Jews. While I understand that aspect of the book, it's still a very troubling book in the Bible.

In chapter one, Queen Vashti is put away from her royal role for her offence in refusing the king's order to put her beauty on display for him and his apparently drunken group of guests. We also see the start of King Ahasuerus being easily swayed by whoever has his ear at the time. Memucan tells the king that he needs to act to reprove the queen, otherwise the wives of the nobles and princes will decide that they don't need to jump at the whims of their husbands.

In chapter two, we have the Persian equivalent of *The Bachelor* in the form of a prolonged beauty contest to find the king a new bride—except that the king was not a bachelor at that time. We aren't told how many *"fair young virgins"* (2:3) were compelled to audition before the king, but apparently there were quite a few (2:13–14). Chapter two ends with Esther supplanting Vashti as the queen.

Chapter three finds Haman bending the king's ear, and the king casually agreeing to a plan to exterminate an entire race of people, the Jews, on a whim and an offer of money for the treasury. As a Gentile, I find myself asking if the entire problem might have been prevented had Esther informed the king that she was Jewish rather than heeding Mordecai's instructions to keep this a secret (2:20). If Esther had given this information to her husband, might Haman have either refrained from his evil plan in the first place, or merely have been rebuffed by the king? Instead, chapter four has a somewhat reluctant Esther agreeing to Mordecai's request to take steps to save their race from extinction.

Chapter five sets the stage for the balance of the book. Esther arranges for the banquet with the King, and Haman starts work on his gallows for his rival, Mordecai. We aren't told why Haman couldn't simply wait the few days for the edict against all Jews to take effect.

Chapter six might be the shining light of the book, as the king finally honours and elevates Mordecai—but this only happens on a whim, when the king's servants remind him that he hadn't done anything to reward Mordecai for saving his life.

In chapter seven, Esther turns the tables on Haman. Chapters eight and nine are the terrible but predictable outfall of a legal system in which the king can't rescind his own decrees. Unable to delete the order to extinguish the Jews, all Ahasuerus can do is authorize the Jews to fight back. Predictable bloodshed ensues, and Esther even makes sure that Haman's sons are executed.

The very short chapter ten is essentially a case of "all's well that ends well"—provided that you ignore the bloodshed, the unfortunate fate of Queen Vashti, and the numerous fair young women who did not win *The Bachelor*. All in all, I don't find this an easy book to read, apart from the fact that God ultimately saves and preserves His people.

APPLICATION FOR TODAY:

Be very careful who has your ear and which suggestions you accept! You have the mind of Christ.

18

JOB 3:16

PREFACE: THIS VERSE IS a small part of a fairly long chapter in which Job laments the fact that he was even born. The lament starts at verse eleven, so I've included part of that verse:

> *Why did I not die at birth?* (v. 11, NKJV)

> *Or why was I not hidden like a stillborn child, like infants who never saw light?"*
> (v. 16, NKJV)

KEY MESSAGE:
GOD KNOWS MORE THAN WE DO. TRUST HIM.

The book of Job is about a man who suffers every misfortune imaginable and is crying out to God, seeking an explanation. Early in the book, Job suffers the loss of all his children, his wealth and possessions, and even his health. Only his wife survives, and her unsupportive suggestion to her husband is that he should simply *"curse God, and die"* (2:9). Job responds in kind, telling her that she speaks *"as one of the foolish women speaketh"* (2:10). (I don't recommend this book as an ideal example of how to have a conversation with your spouse.)

Job's wife's lack of encouragement and support is then matched by the arrival of three of Job's friends (which ultimately becomes four friends with the sudden appearance of Elihu in Job 32). None of them offer Job much in the way of encouragement. Instead, they each take turns expounding their own explanation for Job's misfortune. Each of them is spectacularly wrong, to the extent that when God ultimately speaks (Job 38–42), the Lord tells the friends (42:7–8) that they need to make sacrifices to God and ask Job to pray for them.

Chapter three shows us that the lament to wish one had never been born at all has been part of human existence for a long time—well before Queen gave us "Bohemian Rhapsody." Among the messages we take from Job is that God knows far more than we do, and He doesn't owe us any explanation for what happens to us. It's up to us to acknowledge God and seek His path. This isn't always easy. Many years ago, I attended the funeral service for a young man who'd been killed in a motorcycle accident. His father was a real man of God who worked with Wycliffe Bible Translators, and he gave the eulogy. He said that many people had asked him how God could have taken his son at such a young age. He then responded that those people had the wrong perspective. He said that in his son's life, there had been many dangers and difficult situations, and that God didn't take his son at age sixteen; rather, God had preserved his son for sixteen years and allowed the family the joys of growing together. I doubt many of us could have that perspective. I'm fairly certain that I couldn't have done so.

At the end of Job, the Lord restores Job's wealth and gives him twice as much as he had before (42:10). Job and his wife go on to have seven sons and three daughters (42:13). But God didn't owe anything to Job. He wasn't duty-bound to honour Job's faithfulness. From a human perspective, it always bothered me that the book seems to adopt an "all's well that ends well" position, even though Job's original children (seven sons and three daughters) are obviously still dead. However, in doing so, I risk assuming the role of Job's friends instead of understanding the key message of the book.

APPLICATION FOR TODAY:

There only is one God, and you are not the one! Seek God's face and His wisdom, but understand that He does not owe you an explanation.

19

PSALM 3:8

WHILE SOME OF THE psalms are very long, Psalm 3 ends with verse eight, which says this:

> *Salvation belongs to the Lord. Your blessing is upon Your people.* (NKJV)

KEY MESSAGE:
SALVATION BELONGS TO THE LORD.

I can't improve upon the succinct message in the verse itself.

Some translations of the Bible provide this preface to Psalm 3: "A Psalm of David when he fled from Absalom his son." The lives of both Job and David are stories of increase, loss, and restoration. While Job suffered the unexpected deaths of his children, David had what can only be described as an extremely dysfunctional family. One of his sons (Amnon) raped his half-sister (Tamar) and then rejected her. He in turn was killed by one of his half-brothers, Absalom. As noted in the preface to this psalm, Absalom decided that he would make a better king than his father, so he rebelled against him. For a time, Absalom had the upper hand, and David was forced to flee. In the end, however, the Lord's anointed king (David) prevailed, because salvation belongs to the Lord. God worked through human agents to cause Absalom to reject the advice of Ahithophel in favour of the deliberately misleading advice proffered by Hushai, who was an early example of a double agent! (See 2 Samuel 16–18.)

While there are differences between the Old Testament and the New Testament, this truth remains constant: there is one Lord, and He alone offers salvation. As the apostle Peter said when he addressed the Sanhedrin: *"Nor is there salvation in any other, for there is no other name under heaven given among men by which we must be saved"* (Acts 4:12, NKJV).

The heading for this psalm in my copy of the New King James Version is this: "The Lord helps His troubled people." This too is a constant truth upon which we can rely. So if you haven't sought salvation from the Lord, you need to do that as a prelude to seeking anything else from God. The Lord helps His troubled people, so if you're in need of His help, first ensure that you are in fact one of His people. Acknowledging the Lord is the start of everything in your life.

APPLICATION FOR TODAY:

God still offers salvation and help to His people. He is the same yesterday, today, and forever!

20

PROVERBS 3:16

[Referring to Wisdom] Length of days is in her right hand, and in her left hand riches and honour.

KEY MESSAGE:
WE SHOULD SEEK WISDOM, AND TRUE WISDOM COMES FROM GOD.

THE BOOK OF PROVERBS spends a lot of time discussing and describing wisdom. According to *Strong's Exhaustive Concordance of the Bible,* which laboriously recounts every word found in the King James Version of the Bible, the book of Proverbs has fifty-four mentions of the word "wisdom," and another sixty-five of the word "wise." This adds up to almost four references for each chapter in the book. The full discussion of wisdom is longer than that of course, since many verses contain an extended discussion of the topic. For example, today's subject verse doesn't actually contain the words "wisdom" or "wise" because this section begins with verse thirteen: *"Happy is the man that findeth wisdom, and the man that getteth understanding."*

While some of the verses, taken in isolation, might sound as though they are merely an abstract personification of an elusive target, the Bible makes it clear to a diligent reader that God is the source of all true wisdom. For example, the oft-quoted verses five and six in this chapter tell us to: *"Trust in the Lord with all thine heart, and lean not unto thine own understanding. In all thy ways acknowledge him, and he shall direct thy paths."* Verse nineteen informs us that: *"The Lord by wisdom hath founded the earth; by understanding hath he established the heavens."*

In our world today, wisdom is in short supply, and many aren't interested in seeking what God has to say to them. They're more interested in social media and the latest words from an "influencer," someone who is often less equipped than the seeker to supply wisdom. To truly seek the Lord's wisdom, we need to start with the Bible. God's Word is free of error, and He's willing to teach all who truly seek after Him. The New Testament book of James tells us how to begin this process. In James chapter one, verses five through seven, he writes:

> *If any of you lack wisdom, let him ask of God, that giveth to all men liberally, and upbraideth not; and it shall be given him. But let him ask in faith, nothing wavering. For he that wavereth is like a wave of the sea driven with the wind and tossed. For let not that that man think that he shall receive anything of the Lord.* (James 1:5–7)

APPLICATION FOR TODAY:

Seek wisdom from God. He is still willing to instruct us!

21

ECCLESIASTES 3:16

And moreover I saw under the sun the place of judgment, that wickedness was there; and the place of righteousness, that iniquity was there.

KEY MESSAGE:
LIFE IS A COMPLEX PUZZLE. APART FROM GOD, IT WILL NEVER MAKE SENSE.

THE BOOK OF ECCLESIASTES has fascinated and troubled readers for many years. It's a book that is often quoted. For example, Ernest Hemingway derived the title for his classic novel *The Sun Also Rises* from Ecclesiastes 1:5. He even prefaced the novel with a long quotation taken from verses four through seven of that chapter. The first nine verses of chapter three are also well known, since they form the lyrics for the song "Turn! Turn! Turn!" The music was written by Pete Seeger, who adapted the lyrics from the Bible. The song was made popular by the rock group The Byrds in the 1960s. Verse seventeen, immediately following today's subject verse, is really the conclusion of the song, although it doesn't form part of the lyrics. It reads as follows: *"I said in mine heart, God shall judge the righteous and the wicked: for there is a time for every purpose and for every work."*

I suspect that Pete Seeger—and many of those who enjoy his song—didn't actually want to consider the fact that God will ultimately judge us. Rather, the song tries to be a source of comfort and faith that human effort will somehow solve our problems. To that end, Seeger included the parts of the passage that appealed to him, such as *"To everything there is a season"* (v. 1) and either omitted or added to portions that did not appeal. For example, he inserted a line to suggest that human effort could lead to peace. Readers of the passage will note that the concept of people somehow creating peace doesn't actually appear in the Bible. On the contrary, as today's verse informs us, there will be wickedness under the sun, and iniquity even in the place of righteousness. If we are to move forward from trying to create some form of human justice to truly seeking biblical justice, we need to commit to implementing God's instructions as set forth in the Bible.

God will judge each of us and all of our activities in His perfect timing, and our first step is to admit that we fall woefully short of His standard for justice. Only by trusting in the redemptive work of Jesus Christ can we be pure at the judgment day. Once we accept the offer of salvation from Jesus, we need to move forward as His agents of biblical justice on this earth, seeking to expose the wickedness and iniquity in this world so that His kingdom might truly come to earth.

APPLICATION FOR TODAY:

The world is wicked, and the only hope lies in God.

22

SONG OF SOLOMON 3:11

CHAPTER THREE OF THE Song of Solomon ends at verse eleven, which reads this way:

> *Go forth, O daughters of Zion, and see King Solomon with the crown with which his mother crowned him on the day of his wedding, the day of the gladness of his heart.* (NKJV)

KEY MESSAGE: GOD INTENDED LOVE TO BE PURE AND PASSIONATE IN MARRIAGE.

This book has proved challenging for many commentators, and I'm certainly not the one who will make it clear and easy to follow. Commentators summarize the book as being (a) a portrait of perfect love within marriage and (b) an allegory of the love between God and his bride, the Church. In some Bibles, the editors have inserted headings that purport to identify the various speakers in the book, with the aim of adding some clarity for the reader, for example: "The speaker and audience are identified according to the number, gender, and person of the Hebrew words. Occasionally, the identity is not certain."[2] In this edition of the Bible, the verse I quoted is in a section attributed to the bride of Solomon.

Some editions of the Bible include passages attributed to other women as a sort of chorus. In this edition of the NKJV version, the editors describe them as "the daughters of Jerusalem." However, I recall hearing a speaker discuss this book and say: "If you read what is actually taking place between Solomon

---

[2] *NKJV Large Print Personal Size Reference Bible* (Nashville, TN: Holman Bible Publishers, 2013), 833.

and his bride, I very much doubt that there would have been other people present at the time!"

Even our subject verse presents challenges, although it could be understood as a metaphor or an allegory. We know that Solomon's mother was Bathsheba, and that he was the second child born from the union of David and Bathsheba. Their first son, conceived as a result of the adultery between the couple, died in infancy as part of God's judgment for their sin (see 2 Samuel 12). However, there's no biblical record that Bathsheba ever gave her son a crown, or that she was present on his wedding day. Moreover, Solomon's approach to marriage was (to be charitable) ungodly and based on political alliances. As far as we know, his first marriage was to the daughter of Pharaoh (1 Kings 3:1). In his later life, Solomon went on to have seven hundred wives and three hundred concubines (1 Kings 11), which hardly paints a picture of pure love in marriage. As one might expect, these marriages with foreign women who worshipped false gods caused Solomon to start to follow their gods, and *"his heart was not loyal to the Lord his God, as was the heart of his father David"* (1 Kings 11:4, NKJV).

Some editions of the Bible suggest that the bride referred to is a Shulamite woman: *"Return, return, O Shulamite; return, return, that we may look upon you!"* (6:13, NKJV). While this might be correct, this verse is the only mention of a Shulamite in the entire Bible. In other words, while we're told about the large number of women Solomon married, the Bible doesn't specifically say that he ever married a Shulamite woman.

In conclusion, I regret that I can't offer much insight into this book or the subject verse. I think the best I can do is offer the Song of Solomon to you as a book about the pure and passionate love that should be the hallmark of a godly marriage. Look to the words and sentiments expressed in the book, but don't emulate Solomon's poor and ungodly conduct in his later years.

APPLICATION FOR TODAY:

God intends marriage to be pure and holy, with love expressed without reservation.

23

ISAIAH 3:16–17

The Lord said: Because the daughters of Zion are haughty and walk with outstretched necks, glancing wantonly with their eyes, mincing along as they go, tinkling with their feet; the Lord will smite with a scab the heads of the daughters of Zion, and the Lord will lay bare their secret parts. (RSV)

KEY MESSAGE:
GOD SEES EVERYTHING WE DO, WHETHER GOOD OR BAD.

ISAIAH IS A VERY long book (sixty-six chapters) and covers a huge range of topics. Some verses are well-known and much-loved prophecies of the Messiah (e.g., Isaiah 53, which is the passage the Ethiopian was reading in Acts 8 and from which Philip preached to him). However, there are also many passages of God's judgment upon sin, including these verses for today.

In this chapter, God brings His charges against His people and tells them of their pending judgment. While these particular verses target the women, all of His people are guilty. In verse eight we hear that Jerusalem has stumbled and Judah has fallen *"because their speech and their deeds are against the Lord, defying his glorious presence"* (RSV). The chapter ends with this grim pronouncement: *"Your men shall fall by the sword and your mighty men in battle. And her gates shall lament and mourn; ravaged, she shall sit upon the ground"* (3:25–26, RSV).

Today, many people don't like the idea of God judging them, but their antipathy doesn't alter reality. God has proclaimed the ways in which He expects people to behave. If you choose to reject His commands and guidance, He will judge you. However, as this chapter shows, judgment doesn't come without a warning and an opportunity to repent. While these verses are from the Old Testament, God's standards haven't changed. Today, we have the benefit of a saviour in the person of Jesus Christ. No one will be able to say that he or she didn't know that God had a standard they failed to meet.

APPLICATION FOR TODAY:

God sees all of our sins and will display them in high definition when He judges us. Jesus Christ offers us the perfect cleansing from all of our sins.

24

JEREMIAH 3:16-17

"Then it shall come to pass, when you are multiplied and increased in the land in those days," says the Lord, "that they will say no more, 'The ark of the covenant of the Lord.' It shall not come to mind, nor shall they remember it, nor shall they visit it, nor shall it be made anymore. At that time Jerusalem shall be called The Throne of the Lord, and all the nations shall be gathered to it, to the name of the Lord, to Jerusalem. No more shall they follow the dictates of their evil hearts." (NKJV)

KEY MESSAGE:

BOTH STRAYING FROM GOD AND RETURNING TO GOD HAVE CONSEQUENCES. CHOOSE WHICH CONSEQUENCES YOU WISH TO RECEIVE!

BEING CALLED BY GOD to be a prophet in the days of the Old Testament was a difficult assignment. It often consisted of telling the people that they were sinning against God, calling for repentance, and being ridiculed or ignored. In the case of Jeremiah, he was placed in the stocks for bringing a message that the people didn't want to hear (see Jeremiah 20). Jeremiah lamented that his message made him "*a reproach and a derision daily*" (20:8). However, he went on to say that the word of the Lord was like a burning fire inside of him, and he couldn't hold it back.

Jeremiah 3 records the prophet's early call for the people to repent. Verses fourteen through eighteen show that the Lord's message was not merely a case of telling the people all that they were doing wrong; He also promised them the benefits of returning to true faith in God. In verse fourteen, God proclaims that He is married to His people. In verse fifteen, He says that He will give the people faithful shepherds who will feed them with knowledge and understanding. Verses sixteen and seventeen set out the further promise of obedience to God: the people will no longer even need to worship at the ark of the covenant, because the entire city of Jerusalem will be the Throne of the Lord, and all nations shall be gathered to it.

Despite these clear instructions, the people were unwilling to give up their sinful ways and return to God. They apparently believed that since they were God's chosen people, merely going through formal observances of worship would be sufficient for God to bless and protect them. But God sees past the outward actions and into the heart. The people were so rebellious that by chapter fourteen, God was telling Jeremiah *not* to pray for the people because He wouldn't listen to their prayers, hear their cries, or accept their offerings (14:11–12). At the start of chapter fifteen, one might say that God doubles down on His earlier declaration: He tells Jeremiah that even if Moses and Samuel stood before Him, His mind would not be favourably disposed toward the people.

Today, many people mock the idea of God's judgment and wrath. Similar to the children of Israel in Jeremiah's time, they want to believe that a loving, benevolent God will look past their sinful ways and lustful hearts and bless them anyway because He is loving. But that's not reality. God's standard is holiness, and He doesn't tolerate sin. But He has chosen not to leave us helpless in our sins. He has provided us with the Old Testament prophets such as Jeremiah to clearly explain how to act as His people, and He has provided His own Son, Jesus Christ, to be the atoning sacrifice for our sins. No one will be able to blame God when they end up in hell because they chose their own sinful lusts over the clear words from God.

APPLICATION FOR TODAY:

God's standards are not a mystery. We choose to ignore them at our peril.

25

LAMENTATIONS 3:16

He [God] has also broken my teeth with gravel, and covered me with ashes.

(NKJV)

KEY MESSAGE:

FOLLOWING GOD ISN'T ALWAYS EASY, BUT IT'S ALWAYS THE RIGHT CHOICE.

THE BOOK OF LAMENTATIONS is also attributed to Jeremiah, who is sometimes called "the weeping prophet." In Lamentations 3, Jeremiah sets out his anguish and hope. This is a fairly long chapter at sixty-six verses, although many of the verses are short and remind us of the style seen in books such as Psalms or Proverbs. In verses one through twenty-one, the prophet sets out how his calling as a prophet is extremely difficult: *"He has hedged me in so that I cannot get out; He has made my chain heavy"* (3:7, NKJV).

Even in his anguish, Jeremiah sounds a note of hope. We see the tone shift in verses twenty and twenty-one, where he says that his soul still remembers; therefore, he has hope. Verses twenty-two through twenty-four gave the inspiration for the hymn "Great Is Thy Faithfulness." In Lamentations 3:31–32, Jeremiah declares that the Lord *"will not cast off forever. Though He causes grief, yet He will show compassion ..."* (NKJV). In verse forty, he reminds us that we are the ones who need to *"search out and examine our ways"* (NKJV) and turn back to the Lord.

In the concluding verses, Jeremiah asks the Lord to repay his enemies for their unmerited attacks upon him. In the end, he is confident of God's mercy and protection, despite his current trials.

APPLICATION FOR TODAY:
We are not assured of an easy road because we obey God, but we always have the assurance that He is with us.

26

EZEKIEL 3:16–17

And it came to pass at the end of seven days, that the word of the Lord came unto me, saying, Son of man, I have made thee a watchman unto the house of Israel: therefore hear the word at my mouth, and give them warning from me.

KEY MESSAGE:
SOMETIMES WE NEED TO WAIT UPON THE LORD BEFORE WE HEAR HIM SPEAK TO US.

IN EZEKIEL 1, THE author sets the stage for us: he was a priest, and he was among the captives in exile, sitting by the river Chebar. Suddenly, he began to see visions of God. As the book unfolds, Ezekiel often finds himself carried away by the Spirit of God. In Ezekiel 3, he tells us that the Spirit lifted him up (vv. 12, 14), and entered into him and set upon his feet (v. 24).

Verses fifteen through twenty-one expand upon how God called Ezekiel. The priest sat among the exiles by the river for seven days, *"astonished"* (v. 15), before he heard from God. It was then that God gave him his assignment. Ezekiel was to be a watchman who would bring God's message to the people. He was to communicate clearly and precisely what God told him to say. If Ezekiel failed to communicate the message to a wicked person, with the result that the person did not repent, God would hold Ezekiel to account for that failure. However, if he faithfully set out God's word and the person failed to repent, Ezekiel would be blameless, and the other person would bear the consequences of his sins (3:18–19). God also informed the priest that there would be periods of time when He wouldn't allow him to speak at all: *"I will make thy tongue cleave to the roof of thy mouth"* (3:26). But when God again directed him to speak, he needed to do so (3:26–27).

While God's instructions were clear, He also told Ezekiel not to expect a favourable reception from the people. God noted that He wasn't sending His messenger *"to a people of a strange speech and of an hard language"* (3:5) but rather to His own people, the house of Israel. Nevertheless, God told Ezekiel that the people would not listen to his message, because *"they be a rebellious house"* (3:9). God also calls His people *"impudent and hardhearted"* (3:7). However, God tells Ezekiel not to be afraid of the rejection he will face, because God has strengthened him for the task and will be with him throughout.

In addition to the verbal messages Ezekiel was to communicate, God had him use illustrations at various times. Many of these were onerous, but the priest fulfilled them all. For example, in Ezekiel 4, God instructed him to lie on his left side for 390 days and then to lie on his right side for 40 days, with each day representing one year of the iniquity of Israel.

As you read this book, you'll see patterns emerge. Many chapters begin with the phrase *"the word of the Lord came to me, saying ..."* as Ezekiel begins the account of another message from God. Secondly, Ezekiel is unique among the priests and prophets of the Old Testament in that God consistently refers to him by the phrase *"son of man."* We're familiar with Jesus using this phrase to refer to Himself in the New Testament, but Ezekiel is the only Old Testament character to receive this designation. Finally, God will often let us know to whom a particular message is directed. While most of the words are for the house of Israel, God also directs words to Tyre (Ezekiel 27–28) and to Egypt (Ezekiel 29).

I've been a long-time admirer of Ezekiel. He faithfully fulfilled his very difficult calling for a long time (the entire book is forty-eight chapters long) and was undaunted by the fact that God told him at the outset that the people wouldn't listen to him. No one enjoys being the bearer of what's seen as bad news and then facing rejection. In the end, the book does give us a hopeful vision: *"... the name of the city from that day shall be, The Lord is there"* (48:35).

APPLICATION FOR TODAY:

When God calls us, we are to carry out our assignment faithfully. The results (or lack thereof) are entirely up to God.

27

DANIEL 3:16–18

Shadrach, Meshach, and Abednego answered the king: "O Nebuchadnez'zar, we have no need to answer you in this matter. If it be so, our God whom we serve is able to deliver us from the burning fiery furnace; and he will deliver us out of your hand, O king. But if not, be it known to you, O king, that we will not serve your gods or worship the golden image which you have set up."

(RSV)

KEY MESSAGE:
GOD IS THE ONLY ONE ENTITLED TO, AND WORTHY OF, OUR WORSHIP.

THIS PASSAGE IS PROBABLY one of the best-known stories from the Old Testament. It has been the source of sermons, articles, and songs. It's a strong Old Testament example of the reply *"we must obey God rather than men"* which the apostles gave to the council in Acts 5:29b (RSV). (It's rather ironic that the New Testament answer was given to the Jewish religious leaders, who presumably thought that they were the ones obeying God!)

The three men in our verses were resolute that only God was worthy of worship. It's clear from their answer to the king that they didn't know how the events would unfold that day. They certainly believed that God was fully capable of rescuing them from the fiery furnace, but they didn't presume upon His mercy in that regard. They told the king that even if God didn't deliver them, they still wouldn't bow down to a golden idol.

It's interesting that Nebuchadnezzar didn't ask the men why they were in captivity in Babylon if God was able to deliver them. The answer to that question is that God was in control, even though the king thought he was the one in charge. God had ordained the captivity and exile because His children had been unfaithful, and He needed to chasten and correct them. This is an important part of the lesson for us too. We may not always have easy times, and God may not remove us from every storm. But that doesn't mean He isn't watching over us and in control of circumstances. As Job learned, following God doesn't guarantee an easy or trouble-free life, but it's still the right thing to do, because only God is worthy of our worship, and He will direct our paths.

I also find it remarkable that neither this miracle nor Daniel's interpretation of the king's dream in chapter two appear to have caused Nebuchadnezzar to become a true worshipper of Yahweh. In fact, in Daniel 2:46, we're told that the king *"worshipped Daniel, and commanded that they should offer an oblation and sweet odours to him."* At the end of chapter three, the king does not turn and worship the true God; he merely issues a decree that no one is to speak anything against the God who rescued the three men, because *"there is no other God that can deliver after this sort"* (3:29b).

APPLICATION FOR TODAY:

Worship God and stay faithful. Trust Him, regardless of how the story unfolds.

28

HOSEA 3:4–5

THE BOOK OF HOSEA the prophet has fourteen chapters, but only five have as many as sixteen verses. Chapter three is particularly compact; it ends at verse five. Even these five verses can be divided into two distinct parts. In verses one through three, God tells Hosea that he is to buy back his unfaithful wife, which he does. This is a picture of how God ransoms His unfaithful children, regardless of how many times we go astray. Verses four and five contain a prophetic message for Israel:

> *For the children of Israel shall dwell many days without a king or prince, without sacrifice or pillar, without ephod or teraphim. Afterward the children of Israel shall return and seek the Lord their God, and David their king; and they shall come in fear to the Lord and to his goodness in the latter days.* (RSV)

KEY MESSAGE:
ISRAEL WILL RETURN TO TRUE WORSHIP OF THE LORD.

Hosea 3:4 has been fulfilled and is being fulfilled today: Israel does not have a king or a prince. Israel has not offered sacrifices in the temple since it was destroyed in AD 70. Verse five, however, is yet to occur. The children of Israel have not, as a whole, returned to seek the Lord, although there are small groups of Christian believers in that land. There has been much speculation about when Christ will return and what constitutes the "latter days." Most of this is not productive. Jesus said that no one knows the day or the hour of His return, except for the Father (Matthew 24:36). What we do know is that

Jesus will return, and that the end is getting closer each day. Given that God's timetable is very different from ours, it's certainly probable that the "latter days" could take decades. In his second epistle, Peter said: "*But do not ignore this one fact, beloved, that with the Lord one day is as a thousand years and a thousand years as one day*" (2 Peter 3:8, RSV).

God's Word is true and never fails. Israel will return and seek the Lord their God. While we should be willing to share the good news of Jesus with anyone, we should certainly be alert for opportunities to do so with Jewish people. I'm a graduate of York University in Toronto, and many of my classmates were Jewish. This was my first experience with Jewish people, and it was eye-opening for this sheltered Gentile from Etobicoke! I learned that—as is the case with all of us—you can't take a "one size fits all" approach. Some were faithful observers of the Jewish faith—attending the synagogue, observing the holy days and dietary restrictions, and having minimal contact with non-Jewish students. Others were less strict. I recall one of my classmates saying that how quickly his father recited the Seder at Passover depended upon what time the Toronto Maple Leafs game started that day! Still others were proud of their Jewish heritage but had little interest in observing the faith. I must say that I didn't do very well at engaging with my Jewish classmates, although I improved with time. (I attended the university for seven years, with a four-year undergraduate degree and then a three-year law degree). At one forum, a Jewish student said he rejected Jesus "just as I reject any other false messiah." At the time, it merely made me angry. Today, I would have tried to speak with him and ask him exactly how he had decided that Jesus was a "false messiah." We need to be willing to share our faith with the Jewish people but always with respect and the willingness to hear their stories too.

APPLICATION FOR TODAY:

As God gives you opportunities, be open to discussions with Jewish people.

29

JOEL 3:16

The Lord also shall roar out of Zion, and utter his voice from Jerusalem; and the heavens and the earth shall shake: But the Lord will be the hope of his people, and the strength of the children of Israel.

KEY MESSAGE:
SOMETIMES GOD CAN BE HEARD IN THE "STILL SMALL VOICE" — BUT NOT ALWAYS!

THE BOOK OF JOEL is known mainly for its devastating picture of the plagues of locusts described in chapter one. However, God never leaves us without hope. As the book moves forward into chapters two and three, there are promises of restoration from God. The apostle Peter in his great sermon in the book of Acts quoted Joel 2:28–32, saying that those verses were being fulfilled that day (see Acts 2:16–21).

Chapter three is a picture of God's restoration and vindication of His people. God also promises that He will *"judge all the heathen round about"* (v. 12). The book ends on a note of ultimate triumph in 3:20–21: *"But Judah shall dwell for ever, and Jerusalem from generation to generation. For I will cleanse their blood that I have not cleansed: for the Lord dwelleth in Zion."*

The fact that many today take a stand against Israel shows that they haven't read or understood the Bible. In book after book God's Word is clear: He has given this land, including Jerusalem, to His Jewish people. It is their land and their heritage. Those who oppose Israel are opposing Almighty God, and I can tell you who will win that battle! So the next time you hear such words, consider your response and reaction. Remember, it's not likely that these people are the enemy; it's more likely that they've been deceived by the enemy. In either case, however, Christians should align themselves with God and stand for His Jewish people and their right to possess and thrive in the Holy Land.

APPLICATION FOR TODAY:
God will roar out the message of hope for His people!

30

AMOS 3:15

AMOS 3 ENDS AT verse 15, which is this declaration of judgment from God:

And I will smite the winter house with the summer house; and the houses of ivory shall perish, and the great houses shall have an end, saith the Lord.

KEY MESSAGE:
GOD DOES JUDGE PERSISTENT, UNREPENTANT SIN.

Amos is an interesting character. First of all, he wasn't a prophet or a priest. In Amos 1:1, he's described as *"among the herdmen of Tekoa."* In chapter seven, Amaziah the priest tells him that if he insists on speaking prophecies, he should move to the land of Judah and not speak his words in Bethel. Amos replies:

I was no prophet, neither was I a prophet's son; but I was an herdman, and a gatherer of sycamore fruit: And the Lord took me as I followed the flock, and the Lord said unto me, Go, prophesy unto my people Israel. (7:14–15)

Throughout the book, Amos gives us a constant refrain of the phrase *"thus says the Lord."* He brings the Lord's judgment against a variety of nations, including Damascus, Gaza, Tyre, Edom, Amnon, and Moab. I expect that his audience—made up of the people of Israel—would have been quite pleased with each of these judgments. However, they would have been less receptive when the messages came home to roost.

In Amos 2, he brings God's judgment against Judah, and in chapter three, he speaks to the children of Israel. Amos 3 opens with the Lord reminding them that He was the One who delivered them from Egypt. The Lord tells them that He will bring Israel's transgressions back against the people. This book contains little that the people would find encouraging or comforting until we reach the last five verses of the book—Amos 9:11–15. The final verse might be one of the most encouraging things God has spoken to Israel: *"And I will plant them upon their land, and they shall no more be pulled up out of their land which I have given them, saith the Lord thy God."*

APPLICATION FOR TODAY:

No one is beyond God's judgment or out of His reach for restoration if he repents.

31

OBADIAH 1:16

OBADIAH IS A VERY short book—just one chapter of twenty-one verses. It's directed against Edom, not against Israel. In verse fifteen, God tells the people of Edom that their evil deeds will turn back against them: *"As you have done, it shall be done to you"* (RSV). Verse sixteen then reads as follows:

> *For as you have drunk upon my holy mountain, all the nations round about shall drink; they shall drink and stagger, and shall be as though they had not been."* (RSV)

KEY MESSAGE:
CHOOSING TO NEGLECT YOUR SPIRITUAL LIFE WILL CATCH UP WITH YOU.

In verses twelve through fifteen, the Lord reproves Edom with a series of rebukes, which each begin with *"you should not have"* done this: gloated over your brother in his misfortune; rejoiced when Judah suffered misfortune; boasted when they were in distress; gloated over his disaster; looted his goods; denied refuge to fugitives. In short, while Edom chose to ignore the plight of others and even took advantage of it, the Lord was not oblivious to the situation. We often ask why wrongdoers seem to prosper, but we need to remember that God is not bound to our earthly timelines. Rest assured that He is observing, noting all that's going on, and He will judge and deliver in His time, not ours. Indeed, the book ends with this declaration in verse twenty-one: *"Saviours shall go up to Mount Zion to rule Mount Esau; and the kingdom shall be the Lord's"* (RSV).

There is a further lesson for us today. Sometimes we tend to be glad when misfortune strikes those whom we consider evil or undeserving of blessings. This is the very behaviour God condemned in Edom, so we shouldn't expect that He has a different view of this today. We do well to remember Paul's admonition to the Church in Romans 12:19: *"Beloved, do not avenge yourselves, but rather give place to wrath; for it is written, 'Vengeance is Mine, I will repay,' says the Lord"* (NKJV). Paul is quoting from Deuteronomy 32:35. When we see commands or instructions that appear in both the Old Testament and the New Testament, we should pay particular attention. Paul concludes that chapter by advising his readers to *"overcome evil with good"* (Romans 12:21, NKJV).

APPLICATION FOR TODAY:

Do not despair when evil deeds seem to go unpunished. God is not on your timetable.

32

JONAH 3:10

THE BOOK OF JONAH consists of four relatively short chapters. Only chapter one exceeds eleven verses. The final verse of chapter three is verse ten, which reads as follows:

> *And God saw their works, that they turned from their evil way; and God repented of the evil, that he had said that he would do unto them; and he did it not.*

KEY MESSAGE:
GOD'S GRACE EXTENDS TO ALL PEOPLE.

Jonah's story is well-known to many of us from our days in Sunday school, largely because of the story of Jonah being swallowed by the big fish. More recently, it was the subject of a VeggieTales segment, including the memorable song "In the Belly of the Whale." We can take a great deal from this book.

First of all, it's a tale of a very reluctant missionary—Jonah. In the first two verses of the book, God calls upon Jonah to go to Nineveh and declare His judgment against that great city. Jonah's response was to try to flee from the presence of the Lord. He rejected God's assignment and ran in the opposite direction. Quite simply, Jonah didn't want to preach God's message to the Ninevites, who were heathen Gentiles. In all likelihood, he didn't want God to extend mercy to them; he wanted them to burn.

The Bible doesn't tell us whether Jonah really believed it was possible to flee from the presence of the Lord, but he certainly gave it his best effort: he went in the opposite direction and boarded a ship bound for Tarshish. In so doing, he actually ended up with the opportunity to extend God's message to his shipmates. A great storm arose, and all of the others on board were terrified. Jonah 1:5 tells us that everyone on board *"cried ... unto his god,"* hoping that his god would deliver them. Where was Jonah in the midst of this crisis? Verse five tells us that he had gone into the ship and was asleep, oblivious to the peril they faced. The captain had to wake Jonah up and get him to join them in crying out for help. The men then cast lots to determine which of them had caused this storm, and the lot fell upon Jonah.

Jonah then confessed that he was trying to run away from God. When the men asked him what to do, he said that they should throw him into the sea, and then God would calm the storm. To their credit, the men didn't immediately take him up on this suggestion. Verse thirteen tells us that they tried very hard to bring the ship to land. Eventually, they agreed with Jonah's plan and cast him into the sea. Immediately, the sea ceased its raging. Jonah 1:16 tells us the result of this unconventional missionary message: *"Then the men feared the Lord exceedingly, and offered a sacrifice unto the Lord, and made vows."* As is the case with many missionaries, Jonah didn't get to see the fruit of his message, because the Lord had prepared a great fish to swallow him up.

Chapter two finds Jonah inside the fish for three days and three nights, praying to God. This time period is significant, because Jesus subsequently used it for an illustration. In Matthew 12 and Luke 11, the religious leaders ask Jesus for a sign. Jesus replies that the only sign they will get will be the sign of Jonah: that just as Jonah was in the belly of the fish for three days and three nights, so He will be in the earth for that period of time. Jesus then tells the leaders that the men of Nineveh shall rise in judgment and condemn them, because the Ninevites repented at the preaching of Jonah, and now *"a greater than Jonah is here"* (Matthew 12:41). Chapter two ends with Jonah's exit from the fish, as God has the fish vomit him onto the land.

In chapter three, Jonah decides to follow God's directions after all. He travels to Nineveh and proclaims God's message of judgment. All of the people, led by their king, repent of their evil. The end result is in the verse quoted for today: God relents and does not destroy them. It always astounds me that the people of Nineveh were so ready to accept God's message and this messenger, but no one is beyond God's reach when God has prepared their heart.

Chapter four shows us Jonah's odd reaction for a missionary. Rather than being excited by the acceptance of his message and God's mercy, Jonah was "*very angry*" (Jonah 4:1). He didn't want God to extend mercy to them, and he actually asked God to let him die! God then had more work to do in Jonah's heart, which He does before the end of the book.

APPLICATION FOR TODAY:

Don't assume that anyone is beyond God's loving reach—and don't ever hope for his or her destruction!

33

MICAH 3:12

MICAH 3 ENDS AT verse twelve, which reads as follows:

> Therefore shall Zion for your sake be plowed as a field, and Jerusalem shall become heaps, and the mountain of the house as the high place of the forest.

KEY MESSAGE:
GOD WILL NOT BLESS A DISOBEDIENT PEOPLE.

A common issue faced by many of the Old Testament prophets was that the people of Israel believed that since they were God's chosen people, He wouldn't punish or judge them. Often we see the prophets working to correct this wrong belief. This attitude is clearly seen in Micah 3:11, which is the culmination of Micah's explanation of why the Lord will judge them. Micah says that the people—particularly the leaders—have become greedy and will only act for tangible rewards. The "*heads ... judge for reward,*" the priests only "*teach for hire,*" and the prophets "*divine for money.*" Despite these transgressions, the people purport to "*lean upon the Lord*" and say: "*Is not the Lord among us? none evil can come upon us.*" Micah then sets out God's judgment in verse twelve, as quoted above: Zion will be plowed as though it were a field, and Jerusalem will be ruined.

Through God's mercy, the story doesn't end with judgment. Micah 4:1 begins the rest of the story:

> But in the last days it shall come to pass, that the mountain of the house of the Lord shall be established in the top of the mountains, and it shall be exalted above the hills; and people shall flow unto it.

Micah 4:2 states that many nations shall go up to the mountain of the Lord and to the house of the God of Jacob. In part, this prophecy has already been fulfilled, in that many nations have come (and are coming) to the God of Jacob. However, as the chapter unfolds, it becomes clear that we aren't in the time of total fulfillment yet. The chapter says that *"nation shall not lift up a sword against nation, neither shall they learn war any more"* (v. 3). Not even the most positive optimist could say we have reached that time yet!

The book of Micah is well-known for two other passages. In Micah 5:2, the prophet proclaims that the Messiah will be born in Bethlehem. The chief priests and scribes of the early New Testament times knew this prophecy, because they told King Herod that this city would be the birthplace of the Messiah (see Matthew 2:6). To their discredit, however, none of them appeared interested enough in this development to go to Bethlehem and see if that prophecy had been fulfilled!

The second well-known verse is found in Micah 6:8: *"He has shewed thee, O man, what is good; and what doth the Lord require of thee, but to do justly, and to love mercy, and to walk humbly with thy God?"* That verse is still an excellent guide for how we can act in ways that will be pleasing to God.

APPLICATION FOR TODAY:
Do not presume upon God's grace if you aren't seeking to walk in His ways.

34

NAHUM 3:16
Your traders are more than the stars in the sky, but like locusts, they strip the land and then fly away. (NCV)

KEY MESSAGE:
EACH NEW GENERATION NEEDS TO BE TOLD TO FOLLOW GOD AND OBEY HIM.

AS WAS THE CASE with Jonah, the prophet Nahum gave his message to the people of Nineveh. Unlike Jonah, the Bible doesn't give any indication that Nahum was reluctant to proclaim God's message to the city. Nahum spoke his message approximately one hundred years after Jonah, and to some extent, Nahum got to tell Nineveh what Jonah had wanted to tell them: God's judgment is upon you! However, even in Nahum's message, he reminds the people that God doesn't want to destroy anyone.

In Nahum 1:3, he tells them that the Lord is slow to anger; however, He is also great in power and won't at all acquit the wicked. In verse seven, Nahum says that *"The Lord is good, a strong hold in the day of trouble; and he knoweth them that trust in him."* However, Nineveh's time for grace and mercy had come and gone. It's not clear how long the new attitude of repentance we saw in Jonah's day lasted, but clearly it was long gone by Nahum's time. By Nahum 3:5, the Lord tells the people that He is against them and *"will shew the nations thy nakedness, and the kingdoms thy shame."*

Lest there be any doubt that God's time for mercy has passed, chapter three goes on to detail the sins of the city of Nineveh, part of which is seen in verse sixteen, quoted above. The book moves to its climax in verse nineteen: *"Nothing can heal your wound; your injury will not heal. Everyone who hears about you applauds, because everyone has felt your endless cruelty"* (NCV).

This prophecy was fulfilled. Nineveh was overthrown and so badly crushed that its ruins weren't even found until 1842.

APPLICATION FOR TODAY:

God does not delight in punishing our sins, but we do need to genuinely seek to follow Him.

35

HABAKKUK 3:16

When I heard, my belly trembled; my lips quivered at the voice: rottenness entered into my bones, and I trembled in myself, that I might rest in the day of trouble: when he cometh up into the people, he will invade them with his troops.

KEY MESSAGE:
GOD'S ANSWER MIGHT SURPRISE US, BUT WE NEED TO TRUST IN HIM.

TO PUT IT MILDLY, this verse doesn't exactly present an optimistic picture. Stay tuned, however, because the prophet's tone is about to take a dramatic shift. Before we get there, we need to recap what happens in this little book of three chapters.

The book opens with Habakkuk's complaint to God. The prophet asks God how long he must ask for help. In Habakkuk 1:5–11, God gives the prophet a shocking answer. The Lord informs Habakkuk that He is going to use the Babylonians, a *"cruel and wild people"* (1:6, NCV), to bring His people to repentance. This is followed by what some editions of the Bible refer to as Habakkuk's second complaint. Essentially, the prophet goes back to God and says: "What are you talking about? The Babylonians are much worse than we are!" Early in chapter two, the Lord answers. Habakkuk 2:4 is often quoted and is said to be a key verse that inspired Martin Luther. God calls on Habakkuk (and us) to trust in Him, and He assures the prophet that *"the just shall live by his faith."* This verse is quoted in Romans 1:17, Galatians 3:11, and Hebrews 10:38.

In chapter three, Habakkuk moves from complaining to praying. He moves from fear to faith. While verse sixteen, taken on its own, might seem to be a lament of resignation or defeat, the final three verses of the book show that the prophet has full confidence in God. In verses seventeen and eighteen, he says that while various crops might fail (he mentions figs, grapes, and olives), and while the livestock (sheep and cattle) might disappear, he will still be glad in the Lord and have joy in the God of his salvation. He ends in verse nineteen by declaring that the Lord is his strength and will enable him to walk on high places.

There are important lessons for us in this book. First, we need to maintain a holy reverence for God. I'm not sure that many of us today would say we have "trembled" or "quivered" at God's power. Secondly, we need to fully trust in God, even when His answers perplex us. Thirdly, we don't need to be afraid to bring our deepest concerns and cries to God. He is well able to hear and respond, and He is always gracious.

APPLICATION FOR TODAY:
Come to God in reverence and in faith, and listen carefully for His answers.

36

ZEPHANIAH 3:16

In that day it shall be said to Jerusalem, fear thou not: and to Zion, let not thy hands be slack.

KEY MESSAGE:
GOD COMFORTS AND RESTORES HIS PEOPLE.

IN SOME WAYS, THIS book is similar to Habakkuk. Both of them are relatively short—just three chapters. Also, they each begin with the message that God will judge His sinful people. In the case of Zephaniah, the message might be even more pointed and direct than in Habakkuk. In Zephaniah 1:2, we read: "*I will utterly consume all things from off the land, saith the Lord.*" Lest there be any ambiguity in those words, verse three goes on to say, "*I will consume man and beast; I will consume the fowls of the heaven and the fishes of the sea ...*" As the chapter unfolds, God points to complacency among His people. In verse twelve, He notes that there are those in Jerusalem who have said that God will not act at all: "*I will punish those who are satisfied with themselves, who think, 'The Lord won't help us or punish us'*" (NCV).

In Zephaniah 2:1–3, God calls on the people to repent before it's too late. He urges them to seek meekness and righteousness so that they won't be consumed by His judgment. The balance of that chapter shows that God isn't just picking on Israel because they're His children and should know and act better. The chapter speaks of judgment upon the Philistines, the Moabites, the Ammonites, Cush, and Assyria. In short: God will judge the world. This isn't a popular message today. Many people echo the words of complacency set out in the last paragraph: God, if He exists, is out there somewhere and will neither help us nor punish us. We need to muddle along as best we can. This is a pathetic message, and it's not at all what God wants to do for us!

When we return to God, He offers forgiveness and restoration. This can be seen in the concluding verses of this book. Again, it's similar to Habakkuk in that the prophet ends with a song of triumph:

> *At that time I will bring you again, even in the time that I gather you: for I will make you a name and a praise among all people of the earth, when I turn back your captivity before your eyes, says the Lord.* (3:20)

APPLICATION FOR TODAY:
God will judge sin, but He is gracious and offers forgiveness and victory.

37

HAGGAI 2:16

HAGGAI ONLY CONSISTS OF two chapters, and its message is simple and direct: quit fooling around, people! Get busy and rebuild God's temple! In chapter two, God sets out the consequences of the people putting themselves ahead of Him. Simply: they did not fare very well. Haggai 2:16 reads as follows:

> *A person used to come to a pile of grain expecting to find twenty basketfuls, but there were only ten. And a person who used to come to the wine vat to take out fifty jarfuls, but only twenty were there.*
> (NCV)

KEY MESSAGE:
PUT GOD FIRST!

Haggai spoke in the second year that Darius was king (1:1). Darius had granted permission for the Jewish people to return to Jerusalem so that they could rebuild the temple. Some of the people had taken advantage of the opportunity to return home, but they then spent their time building up their own houses. It appears that they hadn't yet even started building the temple, because in chapter one, Haggai brings God's admonition to them: *"Is it right for you to be living in fancy houses while the Temple is still in ruins?"* (v. 4, NCV). Haggai then goes on to set out the consequences of the people's neglect of God. Even the sky was holding back its rain, and the ground wasn't producing crops (v. 10).

The prophet's message had the desired effect. He gave his message on the first day of the sixth month (1:1), and the people began work on the twenty-fourth day of that month (1:15). I'm sure that many of the other Old Testament prophets would have been delighted to obtain such a prompt response. As we have seen, many of them were ignored, abused, or dealt with people who did the exact opposite of what the prophet told them to do!

In chapter two, we can discern that the people needed some ongoing encouragement. The chapter opens one month later—the twenty-first day of the seventh month—with God asking them to recall how great the Temple was before it was destroyed. In Haggai 2:10, God has Haggai involve the priests in a further teaching point. This takes place two months later on the twenty-fourth day of the ninth month. When the people finally complete the work, God assures them that He will bless them (v. 19). The book ends with God's specific promise to Zerubbabel, the governor of Judah, in verses twenty to twenty-three.

APPLICATION FOR TODAY:

If you know that God is calling you to do something, then do it!

38

ZECHARIAH 3:10

ZECHARIAH IS FOURTEEN CHAPTERS long, but chapter three ends with verse ten. That verse reads as follows:

> The Lord All-Powerful says, "In that day, each of you will invite your neighbor to sit under your own grapevine and under your own fig tree." (NCV)

KEY MESSAGE:
BLESSINGS ARE COMING! IT WON'T ALWAYS BE THIS TOUGH.

Zechariah is an extraordinarily positive book. It contains God's promise to restore Jerusalem, as well as many prophecies of events that were fulfilled in Jesus, the Messiah. It's not clear whether the prophet himself understood all of these prophetic words, but I expect he knew they were for a time well into the future. Zechariah 9:9 was fulfilled by the triumphal entry of Jesus into Jerusalem in Matthew 21:5. The words of Zechariah 11:12–13 prophesy about Judas and his betrayal of Jesus, as they refer to the price of thirty pieces of silver and casting the money to the potter. Zechariah 12:10 says that "... *when they look on him who they have pierced, they shall mourn for him, as one mourns for an only child*" (RSV).

Throughout this book there are constant reminders that nothing is too hard for God and that He will bless His people and restore Jerusalem. It's a good book to turn to and read out loud when you need a word of encouragement. It also contains many specific references to Jerusalem. Make no mistake about it: Jerusalem is God's city, and He has ordained it for His people, the Jews.

Any person or group who advocates for anything contrary to this is working for Satan.

APPLICATION FOR TODAY:
God wants to bless His children.

39

MALACHI 3:16

Then those who feared the Lord spoke with one another. The Lord paid attention and heard them, and a book of remembrance was written before him of those who feared the Lord and esteemed his name. (ESV)

KEY MESSAGE:
GOD KNOWS THOSE WHO ARE FAITHFUL TO HIM, AND HE WILL NOT FORGET THEM.

MALACHI IS THE LAST book of the Old Testament. It's a short but important book. Malachi means "my messenger." After Malachi brought these words to the people, it appeared to them that God was silent for a very long time before the Messiah appeared.

Malachi's main purpose was to exhort the people out of their spiritual lethargy. In chapter one, he takes the people to task for offering defective sacrifices to the Lord. God's Word was clear: all animals offered to Him were to be perfect and without blemish. Instead, the people were keeping those animals for themselves and giving God the blind or lame animals. In chapter two, he directs his words to the priests. God tells them in verse two that He will turn their blessings into a curse if they won't honour His name. Chapter two also contains one of the clearest condemnations of the sin of divorce, found in verses thirteen through sixteen. In verse sixteen, God says that He *"hates"* divorce.

As we move into chapter three, God promises the people *"Return to me, and I will return to you"* (v. 7, ESV). God tells the people that they have defrauded Him by not bringing their full tithes and contributions to Him. He explains that such actions are robbing Him: "*Ye are cursed with a curse: for ye have robbed me, even this whole nation*" (3:9). God promises that if they do their part and honour Him, He will "*open you the windows of heaven, and pour you out a blessing*" (v. 10) so that there won't even be room to receive it. In short, we're called to be generous and faithful in giving to God, and God is no man's debtor. The result of Malachi's message is seen in verse sixteen, quoted above. God took note of those who feared the Lord and made a decision to change their ways. In turn, He promised to remember and protect those who truly returned to Him and served Him.

Chapter four is short—just six verses—but powerful as Malachi's message comes to its conclusion. God says that He will burn up those who continue to walk in wickedness and that nothing will remain of them. He again promises healing and restoration to those who are faithful. Verse two gives us the reference to the Sun of righteousness rising with healing in His wings, which has been made popular in verse three of the Christmas carol, "Hark the Herald Angels Sing." Verse five says that God will send Elijah the prophet before the coming of the day of the Lord. When Jesus' disciples asked Him about this, Jesus replied that Elijah had come but the people failed to recognize him—and the disciples understood that He was referring to John the Baptist.

As others have noted, the Old Testament ends with God's warning that He could "*smite the earth with a curse*" if people don't turn to Him, and the New Testament ends with a blessing: "*The grace of our Lord Jesus Christ be with you all. Amen*" (Revelation 22:21).

APPLICATION FOR TODAY:

Examine your heart and consider if there are areas in your life where you need to turn (or return) to God and serving Him.

40

MATTHEW 3:16-17

And Jesus, when he was baptized, went up straightway out of the water: and, lo, the heavens were opened unto him, and he saw the Spirit of God descending like a dove, and lighting upon him: And lo a voice from heaven, saying, This is my beloved Son, in whom I am well pleased.

KEY MESSAGE:
GOD THE FATHER DECLARED THAT JESUS IS HIS SON.

CHAPTER THREE OF MATTHEW'S Gospel tells us about the ministry of John the Baptist. The chapter opens with John beginning his ministry of preaching repentance and baptizing people who wanted to confess and turn from their sins. John was always clear that he wasn't the coming Messiah. For example, in Matthew 3:11–12, he made reference to one coming after him who was mightier than John and would baptize *"with the Holy Ghost, and with fire."*

The baptism of Jesus by John isn't easy for me to understand. Clearly, Jesus didn't need to be baptized for the forgiveness of His sins, because He didn't have any sin in Him. Indeed, when Jesus first approached John, John rebuffed the request. In Matthew 3:15, Jesus replies that John should proceed *"to fulfill all righteousness."* The New Century Version uses the wording: *"Let it be this way for now. We should do all things that are God's will."* I'm not a theologian, so I still struggle with this passage. The best I can do is to note that Jesus was truly man and truly God, and His submission to baptism sets an example for us in both the act of baptism and the mindset of submission to God's will. Further, this passage provides us with an illustration of the three persons of the Holy Trinity. Jesus the Son is baptized, the Holy Spirit descends upon Jesus, and God the Father speaks. This is a fitting illustration for us: be baptized because it pleases God and receive the blessing of the Holy Spirit.

Matthew 3 ends with verse seventeen. Chapter four then begins with the Holy Spirit leading Jesus into the wilderness for forty days, where Jesus is tempted by the devil. Having resisted the temptation and defeated the devil, Jesus begins His ministry and starts calling His disciples.

APPLICATION FOR TODAY:

Repent, be baptized, receive the Holy Spirit, and walk with Jesus.

41

MARK 3:16

And Simon he surnamed Peter.

KEY MESSAGE:
JESUS CALLED HIS DISCIPLES AND KNEW THEM PERSONALLY.

THIS VERY SHORT VERSE comes in a list of the names of Jesus' disciples. The list begins with Peter in verse sixteen and ends with Judas Iscariot in verse nineteen. I heard an interesting sermon about the disciples when we were on vacation in Seattle. Pastor John Leprohon at Eastridge Baptist Church noted that the order in which the disciples are listed is always the same: Peter, James and John (the brothers who were sons of Zebedee), Andrew, Philip, Bartholomew, Matthew, Thomas, James the son of Alpheus, Thaddeus, Simon the Canaanite, and Judas Iscariot (the traitor).

To some degree, this order reflects how much we are told about each of these men, although Judas is well-known due to his betrayal of Jesus. Also, Thomas is known as "doubting Thomas" for his assertion that he wouldn't believe that Jesus had risen from the dead until he saw Jesus in person and could put his hand into the nail holes. But I think most of us would be hard pressed to describe anything significant about Thaddeus or Simon the Canaanite. However, Jesus called each of these men, and they each had a role to play in His ministry. In Matthew 3:14–15, we're told that Jesus ordained each of them and sent them forth to preach. We're also told that He gave them *"power to heal sicknesses, and to cast out devils"* (v. 15). They weren't merely along for the ride!

Each of us is called by Jesus to have a role in His ministry and work. While some us might have more significant roles than others, Jesus knows us each by name and has something for us to do. Don't overlook the seemingly mundane tasks He calls you to perform. It might be as simple as helping a neighbour, or offering a kind word to someone who's having a hard day. In short, if you're certain that Jesus is prompting you to act, you obey.

In *The Penguin Dictionary of Saints*, Donald Attwater notes that Thaddeus is better known as Jude and sometimes referred to as Lebbaeus. He explains that it's possible that he was the writer of the letter of Jude in the New Testament.[3] So we shouldn't be too concerned about our own name or reputation but rather with following God's call upon our lives. The same book notes that Simon the Canaanite is also known as Simon the Zealot (or as *Good News for Modern Man* calls him, "the patriot.") But even the *Penguin Dictionary* says that nothing else is known about him for certain, although it's possible that he preached the gospel in Egypt and Persia.

APPLICATION FOR TODAY:
Obey the call of Jesus upon your daily life. Trust Him for the results.

---

[3] Donald Attwater, *The Penguin Dictionary of Saints* (London, UK: Puffin Books, 1984), 203.

42

LUKE 3:16

John answered, saying unto them all, I indeed baptize you with water; but one mightier than I cometh, the latchet of whose shoes I am not worthy to unloose: he shall baptize you with the Holy Ghost and with fire.

KEY MESSAGE:
JOHN THE BAPTIST PREDICTS THE IMMINENT ARRIVAL OF THE MESSIAH.

IT WOULD HAVE BEEN easy for John to accept the accolades and the glory some people were prepared to offer as they considered whether he might be the promised Messiah. However, John clearly knew that he was not the Messiah. More importantly, he knew who the Messiah was when Jesus appeared before him. (See the entry on Matthew 3:16.) It's also clear that John knew that it wouldn't be long before the Messiah would arrive. It's important to understand our role in the kingdom of God. The apostle Paul reminds us not to think more highly of ourselves than we should. Jesus taught the importance of humility. That doesn't mean that we don't have a role to play; it merely means that God is the One who sets up the roles. To put it in baseball terms: we might want to have the glory of hitting a grand slam home run, but sometimes it's merely our role to put down a sacrifice bunt and advance the runners already on base.

I also find it interesting that John predicted the arrival of the Holy Spirit in conjunction with Jesus. Jesus declared that the Holy Spirit was to be the Comforter who would arrive and never leave His followers, but only after Jesus returned to heaven. This is exactly what happened in Acts 2. It's less clear to me what one makes of John's reference to fire. I believe that it's probably an allusion to the power inherent in Jesus as He began His ministry.

The relationship between Jesus and John had its ups and downs. In Luke 1, Elizabeth says that the unborn child in her womb—the future John the Baptist—leapt for joy when Mary, the mother of Jesus, arrived. Here in chapter three, John knows that Jesus is the Messiah, yet in Luke 7, John sends two of his disciples to Jesus to ask if Jesus really is the coming Messiah. We aren't told what caused John to have his doubts, but this passage should provide some comfort in our own times of doubt.

Jesus' response is one of action: He cured illnesses, cast out evil spirits, and restored sight to the blind. He then tells John's followers to report to John what they had seen. No doubt they would have understood that Jesus had just shown them the actions of the Messiah as foretold in Isaiah 35:5. After the followers of John leave, Jesus speaks about John the Baptist, stating that he is the fulfillment of Malachi 3:1, the messenger who prepared the way for the Messiah.

APPLICATION FOR TODAY:
Ask for God's wisdom in finding and fulfilling the role He has for you each day.

43

JOHN 3:16

For God so loved the world, that he gave his only begotten Son, that whosoever believes in Him should not perish, but have everlasting life.

KEY MESSAGE:
JESUS CAME TO SAVE US, NOT TO CONDEMN US.

ALMOST EVERY CHRISTIAN KNOWS this verse by heart. It has rightly been referred to as "the most precious verse." It also provides the essential answer to anyone who has wondered whether or not he or she has been guaranteed salvation and eternal life. While it's less common today than it once was, there are still some churches that teach that you cannot know for certain whether you will get to heaven. This verse says that you can know that for certain. You are included in *"whosoever."*

Many other religions teach that you can't know if you'll reach heaven, or that you must work hard to seek God's approval. As this verse clearly says, it's faith in Jesus plus nothing else that guarantees us everything.

It's also important to recall that Jesus said these words to Nicodemus, who was a respected Pharisee and a ruler of the Jews (John 3:1). As he told Jesus in John 3:2b, the Jewish leaders knew He was a *"teacher come from God: for no man can do these miracles that thou doest, except God be with him."* The balance of the chapter tells us what Jesus said in reply to Nicodemus; it doesn't tell us how Nicodemus responded. Some commentators have called Nicodemus "a timid convert."

In John 7, Nicodemus speaks up for Jesus to the religious leaders, asking them whether it's right for their law to judge any man without hearing from him and knowing what he's doing. At a minimum, Nicodemus wanted to give Jesus the opportunity to answer the questions of the leaders, but it's not certain that this means he was a convert. The religious leaders had already made their minds up, however. At this meeting, their knee-jerk response was to dismiss Jesus because he had come from Galilee, and no prophet was to come from Galilee. John 19 records that Nicodemus provided the myrrh and aloes to prepare the body of Jesus for burial. The Scriptures don't tell us whether or not Nicodemus also witnessed the resurrection and proceeded with true faith in Jesus. One thing we can know for certain is that if Nicodemus did put faith in Jesus, he was saved for all eternity. Nicodemus was included in *"whosoever."*

APPLICATION FOR TODAY:

Put your faith in Jesus. You are included in *"whosoever."* You can know that you have eternal life.

44

ACTS 3:16

It was faith in Jesus that made this crippled man well. You can see this man, and you know him. He was made completely well because of trust in Jesus, and you all saw it happen! (NCV)

KEY MESSAGE:
THERE IS POWER IN THE NAME OF JESUS.

THIS VERSE IS PART of Peter's impromptu sermon to a crowd that had gathered after the healing of a lame man. Peter and John were going to the Temple for afternoon prayers. A lame beggar had been carried to the gate of the Temple to beg for money from those who were arriving for prayer time. Peter called to the man, and the Bible says that, naturally, the man looked over to him, expecting a donation. Instead, Peter gave the man health and the ability to walk for the first time in his life.

His message was simple: "In the name of Jesus Christ of Nazareth I order you to walk!" Peter then took the man by the hand and pulled him up. The Scriptures say that immediately the man's feet and ankles became strong, and he started walking and leaping and praising God. This is an important part of the account. Since the man had been lame from birth, we might reasonably assume that his legs were withered and atrophied, as they had never been used. But that didn't matter to God! God gave full and perfect healing.

As a result of the healing, a crowd gathered to marvel at this miracle. Peter then preached to them all, including the verse set out above. This resulted in the conversion of about five thousand people (Acts 4:4). It also caused Peter and John to be arrested! Acts 4 tells us that the Temple guards and Sadducees had them arrested. The Sadducees were particularly offended, since they were the sect that didn't believe in the resurrection. Apparently they continued in this belief, even though Jesus had answered their position when He was alive (see Matthew 22:23-34).

The arrest gave Peter and John the opportunity to preach to another audience—the religious leaders. Since the leaders couldn't deny that a miracle had occurred (the formerly lame man was standing before them with the disciples) they contented themselves with ordering the disciples not to speak or teach in the name of Jesus. Peter and John immediately informed the leaders that they couldn't obey this order, because they had a duty to obey God rather than men. It's sad that the religious leaders were more interested in their own positions of power than in the truth, but that's in accordance with human nature. There's also a little rhyme that says, "A man convinced against his will is of the same opinion still."

The name of Jesus remains as powerful today as it was back in New Testament times. God is still the God of power and healing. Place your trust in the One who will never abandon you.

APPLICATION FOR TODAY:
Trust in the powerful name of Jesus!

45

ROMANS 3:16
Destruction and misery are in their ways.

KEY MESSAGE:
CHOOSING TO FOLLOW THE WRONG PATH LEADS TO DESTRUCTION.

WHEN I WORKED AT a large law firm, one of the partners said to me: "The trouble with you is that you see everything as black and white." While I had enough sense not to reply that everything *is* black and white, I certainly consider it an accurate statement. The partner in question went on to become a Justice of the Court of Queen's Bench, where she undoubtedly had to render decisions that were black or white. In some cases, the parties to litigation have mixed success, but in criminal law, I've never seen an accused who was "partly guilty"!

This passage is part of a section in which Paul quotes a number of excerpts and concepts from the Old Testament. His words are very much black or white. Consider the following:

"*There is none righteous, no, not one*" (v. 10).

"*There is none that understandeth, there is none that seeketh after God*" (v. 11).

"*They are all gone out of the way ... there is none that doeth good, no, not one*" (v. 12).

"*Whose mouth is full of cursing and bitterness*" (v. 14).

"*There is no fear of God before their eyes*" (v. 18).

The Bible is clear that we are not capable of saving ourselves. This passage reminds us that we are all under sin—both Jews and Gentiles. Pastor and author Charles Price compared the pull of sin to the pull of gravity.[4] We can try to resist, but even our best efforts will fail.

The good news, which Paul turns to in Romans 3:21–31, is that we have the free gift of righteousness by faith in Jesus Christ. Paul uses the word "righteousness" four times in these verses. He concludes in verse twenty-eight by reminding us that we are *"justified by faith without the deeds of the law,"* regardless of our background or circumstances. Faith in Jesus is an inclusive opportunity, and no one is excluded. If that seems black and white, it is reality.

APPLICATION FOR TODAY:

You need to decide which path you will follow. Only one leads to eternal life.

---

[4] Charles Price, *Experiencing Christ in You* (Toronto, ON: The People's Church), January 28.

46

1 CORINTHIANS 3:16

*Know ye not that ye are the temple of
God, and that the Spirit of God
dwelleth in you?*

KEY MESSAGE:
LIVE SO THAT OTHERS CAN SEE THAT CHRIST DWELLS IN YOU.

A NUMBER OF YEARS ago, our church hosted presentations by "Walk thru the Bible." These interactive sessions took you through the Old Testament and the New Testament and gave you short phrases to help you remember what each book told you about God. For example, the opening words for Genesis were "creation; fall; flood." The phrase for 1 Corinthians was "spanking the saints." In this book, Paul sought to correct the behaviour of those who wanted the benefits of salvation while living as part of the world. That problem is evident in today's society. In 1 Corinthians 3, Paul is quite stern. He opens by saying that the readers are living their lives as carnal beings instead of spiritual beings. While they should be ready to receive the meat of God's Word, he is still having to give them milk (v. 2).

Paul goes on to note that there is a lack of unity among the people. Some were saying "I am in Paul's camp" and others were saying that they were in the camp of Apollos. Paul had to remind them that Paul and Apollos were insignificant; the true foundation for their faith (v. 11) had to be Jesus Christ. Any other foundation would crumble and fall away. This analogy recalls Jesus' parable about the foolish man who built his house upon the sand (Matthew 7:24–27). He ends the chapter by saying that the wisdom of this world is foolishness to God (v. 19), and he reminds them again that they belong to Christ, and Christ belongs to God (v. 23).

This passage also shows that we need to respect all members of our team and not try to pull rank on anyone. Paul speaks highly of Apollos in this letter, and Apollos is one of the people Paul asks to see in his letter to Titus. Yet Apollos was a fairly recent addition to the team. We first meet him in Acts 18:24, where he's called "*an eloquent man and mighty in the Scriptures*" (NKJV). However, the passage says that Apollos was only preaching the baptism of John. It was Aquila and Priscilla who "*explained to him the way of God more accurately*" (18:26, NKJV). But Paul doesn't claim superiority to Apollos or other faithful Christians. On the contrary, he says that God is the One who gave the increase (v. 6).

From this chapter, we clearly see that God wants to make a difference in our daily lives, and that each of us should be willing to grow in our knowledge of God. Others should be able to see that we're different and be drawn to the light of Christ in us. Seek to do all things so that the name of Christ is glorified.

APPLICATION FOR TODAY:
Allow the Holy Spirit to direct your daily walk.

47

2 CORINTHIANS 3:16
Nevertheless, when it [Israel] shall turn to the Lord, the vail shall be taken away.

KEY MESSAGE:
FOR MANY WHO ARE UNSAVED, A VEIL COVERS THE EYES OF THEIR HEART.

IN THIS CHAPTER, PAUL refers to the incident in the Old Testament when Moses had a direct encounter with God upon the mountain. When Moses returned to the people, his face literally shone from the reflected brilliance of the most Holy God (see Exodus 34:29–35). Paul then says that the nation of Israel now has a veil upon its heart, because it hasn't turned to Christ. In this verse, Paul says that when Israel turns to the Lord, that veil is taken away, and the people will know the reality of Christ as God.

Some modern translations expand the concept that Israel has a veil over its eyes by using words such as *"a person"* (HCSB) or "anyone." While this is true, it somewhat misses the point of what Paul is actually saying here. He is specifically talking about his Jewish people. He says that they continue to read Moses and the other Old Testament writers and don't understand that they were pointing to a more glorious day when the Messiah would walk among them. In 2 Corinthians 3:17–18, Paul completes the thought. He says that the Lord is that Spirit, and *"where the Spirit of the Lord is, there is liberty"* (v. 17). He says that when we truly see Jesus for who He is, we are changed *"from glory to glory"* (v. 18) by the Spirit of the Lord.

There are two lessons here for us. First, we need to be alert lest a veil is covering our own understanding of the reality of Jesus. Christ came to offer us abundant life, not meaningless rituals or dry religion! We should be excited to worship God, and leave our Sunday services with a spirit of joy. Secondly, we shouldn't be too quick to decide that someone won't accept the gospel message from us. Unless that person is Jewish, it's unlikely that they're reading the writings of Moses and failing to understand their application. It's far more likely that the person isn't reading Moses or the New Testament, and that we need to start our discussion from the very basics of Scripture.

APPLICATION FOR TODAY:

Pray that God will remove any veil covering your eyes so that you might experience the liberty of Jesus.

GALATIANS 3:16

Now to Abraham and his seed were the promises made. He saith not, And to seeds, as of many; but as of one, And to thy seed, which is Christ.

KEY MESSAGE:
SALVATION COMES THROUGH FAITH IN JESUS CHRIST, NOT IN TRYING TO KEEP THE LAW.

AS A RETIRED LAWYER, I appreciate Paul's detailed legal argument in this chapter. The essence of his submissions is this: you cannot claim any measure of righteousness by doing works under the law. You can only attain righteousness by faith in Jesus Christ, given to us by the promise of God.

Galatians 3:16 is a quote from Genesis 12:7, which is God's promise to Abraham. Paul stresses the importance of a covenant and uses a human example. You don't annul or add to a covenant once it's been signed, sealed, and delivered. God gave Abraham a promise, and God delivered on His promise in the person of Jesus Christ. Paul then describes the law as a *"guardian"* (Galatians 3:24, ESV) until faith could be revealed through Christ. He concludes with a well-known passage that shows that salvation is open to all. There is neither Jew nor Greek; neither slave nor free; no male or female. We are all one in Jesus Christ, which makes us Abraham's children. This is an important passage for a world caught up in validating "inclusivity." Christians are often accused of being exclusive or discriminatory, but we preach the most inclusive of all faiths. No one is turned away, and there's not a list of works or duties you must perform in order to be saved. There is only one entry point: placing your faith in Jesus Christ as your righteousness and entry into God's kingdom.

Unfortunately, some have tried to use this passage as support for the ungodly concept of transgenderism ("no male or female"). There is absolutely no basis to conclude that this passage (or any other passage) endorses the idea that anyone is free to change gender. On the contrary, the basis for transgenderism is simply the lie that Satan told Adam and Eve in the garden: "You shall be as gods." It's the lie that says God could have made a mistake when He chose your gender and created you and that you are at liberty to "fix" God's error by changing your gender to match your own feelings. God doesn't make mistakes. Before He formed you in the womb, He knew who you were to be. This passage actually says that you need to accept who you are as created by God, because He already accepted you as His child when He created you.

APPLICATION FOR TODAY:

You don't need to earn God's approval. He already promised it to you when you accepted His Son as your Lord and Saviour.

49

EPHESIANS 3:16–19

That he would grant you, according to the riches of his glory, to be strengthened with might by his Spirit in the inner man; that Christ may dwell in your hearts by faith; that ye, being rooted and grounded in love, may be able to comprehend with all saints what is the breadth, and length, and depth, and height; and to know the love of Christ, which passeth knowledge, that ye might be filled with all the fulness of God.

KEY MESSAGE:
GOD GIVES US STRENGTH, AND CHRIST DWELLS IN US.

AS IS OFTEN THE case with Paul's writing, Ephesians 3:16 is part of a very long sentence. In the King James Version, the full sentence starts at verse fourteen and ends at verse nineteen. Here, Paul asks that the believers will be strengthened by the Holy Spirit so that they can grasp the extent of Christ's love for them. This was important for these believers, as they faced opposition and persecution, but it's equally important for us today.

Once we understand the extent of Christ's love for us, and Christ truly lives in us through the power of His Holy Spirit, we can be filled with "*all the fullness of God.*" This divine power then can work in us so that we may minister to others. The Holy Spirit is available to us and will provide us with insights to minister effectively. Too often we try to minister in our own strength, but, as has often been said, "you make a very poor Holy Spirit."

It's equally important that, as Paul says, we are "rooted and grounded in love." The ministry and work of a Christian should never start from a critical spirit but from the overflowing love of Christ in us. Too often Christians are portrayed as the critical ones who tell people what not to do instead of seeking to heal their wounds.

APPLICATION FOR TODAY:

Think about God's great love for you and let that fill you as you encounter other people.

50

PHILIPPIANS 3:16

Nevertheless, whereto we have already attained, let us walk by the same rule, let us mind the same thing.

KEY MESSAGE:
EACH OF US IS A WORK IN PROGRESS.

PAUL UNDERSTOOD THAT FOLLOWING Jesus was a process. While we are saved purely by God's grace as soon as we accept Jesus Christ as our Lord and Saviour, the rest of our days should be spent in an effort to draw nearer to Jesus and be more like him. In Philippians 3:12, Paul confesses that he hasn't yet attained the goal, nor is he perfect. In verse fourteen he says, *"I press toward the mark for the prize of the high calling of God in Christ Jesus."* In short, we're called to stand firm in the Lord and move forward.

As is the case with Paul, I know that I have not attained the goal of being the best representation possible of Jesus to others. All too often it's easy to be critical of others, to say an unkind word, or to question someone else's motives. This only seems to have increased in the days of social media, and especially in the time of COVID!

We have Jesus for our example and can look to many of the saints who have passed this way before us. Do not despair when you fall short of the goal; that is part of the process. Keep in mind that you have been saved by grace through faith in Jesus, and our goal is to draw closer to Jesus so that we might draw others to Him.

APPLICATION FOR TODAY:

Following Jesus is a daily walk. We won't attain perfection in this life, but we strive to be more like Him.

51

COLOSSIANS 3:16

Let the word of Christ dwell in you richly in all wisdom; teaching and admonishing one another in psalms and hymns and spiritual songs, singing with grace in your hearts to the Lord.

KEY MESSAGE:
THE CHURCH IS A BODY, AND WE WERE MEANT TO OPERATE TOGETHER.

THIS VERSE FITS IN well with Philippians 3:16. If we are to continue to move forward in the Christian life, it's essential to meet and share with other Christians. There is so much that we can learn from other believers and share with them along the way.

There are a number of interesting components to this verse. First, we note that the word of Christ is to be at home in us and will provide us with all wisdom. This is important! We don't have all the answers, but God does. The Holy Spirit will provide us with God's wisdom and lead us along the path, but we need to take the time to ask God for guidance and to wait patiently for the answer. We also need to be open to hear from other believers. Sometimes God uses the body to provide wisdom for His family. Consider the council described in Acts 15. Some of the early Jewish Christians believed that the Gentile converts needed to be circumcised—in effect, become Jewish—in order for God to accept them. Peter provided a word of God's wisdom that refuted this position and turned the tide of the assembly. Be cautious in accepting well-meaning advice from other Christians, however. Be sure that their comments are really from God and not just their own well-intentioned advice. As a guide, know that God will never direct you to do something contrary to His clear word as expressed in the Bible.

As we are taught, so we should teach. This verse tells us to teach and admonish one another. I suspect that most of us are more inclined to admonish than to teach! If we're to do this properly, we must be grounded and established in the Scriptures ourselves. You can't teach someone what you don't know.

Finally, we see the reference to psalms and hymns and spiritual songs. The Christian walk should be filled with music and joy! We quite literally have a reason to sing with grace in our hearts! God has redeemed us, and we should be singing the good news with grace for all to hear.

APPLICATION FOR TODAY:

Do not forsake assembling together with other Christians.

52

1 THESSALONIANS 4:16

FIRST THESSALONIANS 3 ENDS at verse thirteen, so here is 1 Thessalonians 4:16:

> *For the Lord himself shall descend from heaven with a shout, and the voice of the archangel, and with the trump of God; and the dead in Christ shall rise first.*

KEY MESSAGE:
JESUS WILL RETURN, AND EVERYONE WILL SEE HIM WHEN HE APPEARS.

Chapter four of this epistle sets out this theme: Jesus will return, so live your lives in a holy manner worthy of your calling as His followers. In this chapter, Paul provides instruction in a few key areas of life. He begins with an exhortation to sexual purity (vv. 1–8). These words are even more essential today than when Paul wrote them. In verses five and six, he notes that the Gentiles (i.e., unbelievers) don't even remotely follow the laws of sexual purity, and that remains true in our "anything goes" society. In verses nine and ten, Paul calls for brotherly love, including a request that we show our love by our actions and not merely in words. Verses eleven and twelve remind his audience to continue to work hard. Paul takes up this theme elsewhere, and other commentators have noted that it appears as though some believers had simply stopped working, expecting Christ's return to be imminent. It appears that Paul shared this view to some degree, because in verse seventeen he says that when Christ returns, *"we which are alive and remain shall be caught up together to meet the Lord in the air: and so shall we ever be with the Lord."* However, clearly Paul didn't want his readers to be idle layabouts, merely hoping that Christ would rescue them from this world.

Since Paul's time, many speakers and authors have tried to put a timeline on Christ's return. Usually this is the mark of a cult, but some well-intentioned Christians have fallen into the same trap. Jesus was quite clear in telling His followers that He would return, but that no man knows the day or the hour. This was clearly set out in Jesus' final address to the disciples in Acts 1. They were asking if Jesus would now set up an earthly kingdom, but Jesus told them that they were to await the arrival of the Holy Spirit and then become His witnesses on earth. The fact that Jesus told them that they were to testify of him *"unto the uttermost parts of the earth"* (Acts 1:8) should have made it clear that He would not be returning in the short term.

Today, we know that the task of carrying the gospel to the ends of the earth is still not complete, although many Christian organizations have made great progress in getting there. Until Jesus does return, let us continue to be faithful, holy, and walk as Christ would have us walk.

APPLICATION FOR TODAY:

Jesus will return. Stay faithful.

53

2 THESSALONIANS 3:16
Now the Lord of peace himself give you peace always by all means. The Lord be with you all.

KEY MESSAGE:
JESUS BRINGS US PEACE REGARDLESS OF CIRCUMSTANCES.

AS YOU CAN TELL from the content of this verse, it comes near the end of the epistle. In fact, there are only two more verses in 2 Thessalonians, and they are Paul's closing words. This epistle takes up some of the themes from its predecessor: Jesus will return, but don't speculate on when that day will arrive. In the meantime, carry on and have peace in your hearts.

Many people believe that 2 Thessalonians 2:3-4 point to the antichrist coming before Jesus returns:

> Let no man deceive you by any means: for that day shall not come, except there come a falling away first, and that man of sin be revealed, the son of perdition; who opposeth and exalteth himself above all that is called God, or that is worshipped; so that he as God sitteth in the temple of God, showing himself that he is God.

It's not my intention to join the multitude of Christian commentators who have tried to speculate on who the antichrist might be or when he'll be revealed. Suffice it to say that whenever a new tyrant appears in the world, someone will declare that this must be the antichrist. We are called to focus on Jesus, not the enemy. The enemy has already been defeated. I will say that if one assumes that these verses refer to the appearance of the antichrist, it's wrong to say that

Jesus could return at any time. Paul says that this is not true: Jesus will not return until the antichrist arises and declares that he is God. However, as noted in 1 Thessalonians, this is not an excuse for us to do nothing and wait until Jesus appears. We are called to be His witnesses.

The key message from this verse is that regardless of circumstances, Jesus brings us peace. He is the Lord of peace, and Paul says that He can give us peace *"always by all means."* Jesus isn't limited by circumstances. It has been somewhat disappointing to see Christians dismayed by the COVID-19 pandemic. I understand the uncertainty and the frustration. My wife and I had a trip to Australia cancelled due to the pandemic, and certainly that was heartbreaking. But we need to rest assured that Jesus promises us peace in any circumstances.

APPLICATION FOR TODAY:

Let Jesus bring you peace so that you may be an influence of peace on those around you.

54

1 TIMOTHY 3:16

And without controversy, great is the mystery of godliness: God was manifest in the flesh, justified in the Spirit, seen of angels, preached unto the Gentiles, believed on in the world, received up into glory.

KEY MESSAGE:
THIS IS THE ENTIRE GOSPEL IN ONE VERSE!

THIS IS THE VERSE that first caused me to consider writing this devotional book. It's a great verse that contains the entire gospel message. Because it's a "3:16 verse," it was the first verse to make me wonder what other interesting Bible verses might share this reference number, along with the classic John 3:16.

It's a good memory verse because of its parallel structure, with six short phrases, each of which contains a verb and the object of that verb, joined together by short prepositions. It's also an important verse because it reminds us that the gospel included God becoming flesh, dwelling among us, and becoming accessible to the Gentiles.

It's an interesting verse in that it doesn't seem to be part of the main theme of chapter three, although it's the final verse of the chapter and serves as a conclusion of what the gospel message entails. Chapter three is largely devoted to giving young Timothy instructions about appointing leaders in the church. The King James Version uses the words *"bishop"* and *"deacon,"* terms that are still used in churches that observe a formal liturgical tradition. Some Bible translations use more contemporary wording, such as *"church leaders"* and *"church helpers"* (GNT). I don't think much turns on which words one uses;

these instructions are applicable to those who are chosen for leadership roles in the church.

I haven't considered how some churches say that priests should be celibate, given that these verses refer to bishops (and deacons) as being "the husband of one wife" (vv. 2, 12). On the other hand, my mother was raised in the Russian Orthodox Church, and she told me that their tradition was to read verse two literally, so that priests were required to be married. It seems to me that we need to look to these verses as setting out sound examples of Christian character for all to follow.

Having set out these guidelines, Paul tells Timothy (vv. 14, 15) that he hopes to come to Timothy soon, but if he's delayed, then these instructions will help him administer the congregation (vv. 14–15).

Without further introduction or explanation, Paul ends the chapter with our subject verse. In chapter four, he explains that in the latter times, some will fall away from the true faith and be seduced by false spirits. To that extent, our 3:16 verse might serve as a hinge verse, setting out the essential requirements of a sound gospel faith. We need to believe that Jesus was truly God being made manifest in the flesh, that He was preached unto the Gentiles, accepted as the Saviour, and then received up into glory. We now await His return! If we hold fast to this verse, we aren't likely to fall prey to any seducing spirit!

APPLICATION FOR TODAY:
Live your life holding on to the truths set out in this verse.

55

2 TIMOTHY 3:16–17

All scripture is given by inspiration of God, and is profitable for doctrine, for reproof, for correction, for instruction in righteousness: That the man of God may be perfect, thoroughly furnished unto all good works.

KEY MESSAGE:
ALL SCRIPTURE IS VALUABLE. WE SHOULDN'T DISCARD OR IGNORE ANY OF GOD'S WORDS.

THIS IS ANOTHER WONDERFUL verse with a nice parallel structure for memorization. It's full of little gems. First, we have the admonition that *all* Scripture is given by inspiration of God. This is important, for many writers over the years have wanted to explain away or ignore portions of the Bible that they personally didn't like. We need to understand that Scripture is a gift from God to us. It's not our role to reject any portion of the gift or hide it away in the closet. On the contrary, we need to meditate upon each verse and ask what particular use we are to make of that verse on that day. Sometimes we can read a verse many times and then suddenly see an application for we'd never seen before. This is a great mystery of God's gift to us.

If we aren't sure what use to make of that gift on that day, the balance of the verse gives us some ideas. First of all, it might be "*profitable for doctrine.*" For the most part, it's fairly obvious if a verse is intended to be used for doctrine, although different denominations have stumbled over this point and turned their personal preferences into God's doctrine. Generally, if God intends a principle to be one of doctrine, we'll find it in more than one verse and from more than one writer. We also need to be cautious when reading verses from the Old

Testament. The old covenant was very different from the new one, and generally doctrines contained in both the Old and New Testaments are the ones that apply to our lives today.

Secondly, a verse could be provided "for reproof." We might not like these verses; indeed, we might cringe when we read them, but that's precisely the point. If we behave toward someone with ill-temper and then recall that we're to love our neighbours as ourselves, it's pretty clear that God has a reproof for us. It's up to us to accept the reproof, ask for forgiveness, and seek to get back on track.

Thirdly, we have verses *"for correction."* This might be less of a blow to our ego than reproof. Sometimes we might be slightly off course, and we can miss the target completely if we don't make a course correction. This can occur in situations where we have started down the wrong path but haven't followed it to an unwise destination.

Finally, Paul mentions *"instruction in righteousness."* God is offering a gift to teach us how to be more like Jesus as we move forward.

Verse seventeen completes the thought. The ultimate purpose of the gift of Scripture is to seek to make us perfect. We are to be *"thoroughly furnished in all good works."*

APPLICATION FOR TODAY:

Accept the gift of scripture and maintain a regular schedule of reading God's Word.

56

TITUS 3:15

TITUS IS A SHORT book. The last verse in this letter is 3:15, which reads as follows:

> *All that are with me salute thee. Greet them that love us in the faith. Grace be with you all. Amen.*

KEY MESSAGE:
THE CHURCH IS A FAMILY, AND PERSONAL RELATIONSHIPS MATTER.

Paul generally ends his letters with personal greetings, and this short epistle fits that pattern. In the final verses of this letter, Paul mentions four other believers by name: Artemas, Tychicus, Zenas "the lawyer," and Apollos. Two of these people (Artemas and Zenas) are mentioned only in this epistle, but they were clearly important to Paul.

As a retired lawyer, I'm always encouraged by this positive reference to a lawyer in the Scripture, since Jesus had many harsh words about the doctors of the law He encountered. Apollos we likely recognize as one of Paul's partners in the gospel ministry. He's mentioned in Acts 18 and 19, and is referred to extensively in 1 Corinthians. Tychicus also had a role in Paul's ministry. He is referred to briefly in Acts 20:4, and the subscript found in some versions of the Bible at the end of two epistles (Ephesians and Colossians) indicate that Tychicus was the one who faithfully transcribed Paul's words onto the page so that they could be sent to their readers. This should also encourage us, for even those who work behind the scenes are important to God and have a role in His ministry.

Despite the difficult circumstances Paul faced, he was rarely alone. As noted in this verse, there were other believers with him, and they wanted their greetings to be sent along to Titus. Similarly, Paul wanted those who would be with Titus to know that he was sending his greetings to them. Finally, he concludes with a brief benediction: *"Grace be with you all. Amen."* This is a reminder that words of blessing are important. Sometimes we forget this in our busy age, where text messages and abbreviations dominate our exchanges. Any time we have the opportunity to speak or write to someone, we have an opportunity to bless them. We should always take the time to bestow God's blessing upon those we meet. We are the hands and feet of Jesus, so let's also bring His words to their hearts.

APPLICATION FOR TODAY:
There are no unimportant people in the kingdom. Bless someone today.

PHILEMON 1:16

PHILEMON IS A VERY short and personal letter. It consists of just one chapter of twenty-five verses. Verse sixteen reads as follows:

> *Not now as a servant, but above a servant, a brother beloved, specially to me, but how much more unto thee, both in the flesh, and in the Lord?*

KEY MESSAGE:
GOD'S WISH IS FOR RESTORATION, UNITY, AND FELLOWSHIP.

The background to this epistle is well-known. Paul is writing to Philemon on behalf of Onesimus. Onesimus had been a slave to Philemon but escaped and ran away. He encountered Paul, and it appears that Paul was the one who led him to Jesus. In verse ten, Paul refers to Onesimus as *"my son ... whom I have begotten in my bonds."*

Paul is now asking Onesimus to return to Philemon, and he's asking Philemon to accept him, not merely as a servant, but above a servant—a brother in the Lord. In our modern-day context, there is much that we struggle with in this letter. To some extent, it appears that Paul is endorsing slavery by asking Onesimus to return to his master. However, we need to remember that Paul wasn't going to singlehandedly change the culture and lifestyle of his day. What he's doing here is asking Philemon to receive Onesimus as a brother and "do the right thing." Some infer that Paul is asking Philemon to grant Onesimus his freedom. This might be possible, but I don't think we need to go that far. It's possible that Paul is merely telling Philemon that how he treats this servant needs to be radically different from how one would treat a slave. There is nothing particularly abhorrent about the term "servant." While the term is a bit archaic today, many people employ housekeepers or nannies. Moreover, Paul offers to make good any debt that Onesimus might have owed to Philemon by telling him to *"put that on mine account"* (v. 18).

The key message of the letter is this: God values relationships and restoration. Paul could not, in good conscience, merely keep Onesimus with him and stay silent about the matter. It's likely that Paul would have preferred to escort Onesimus to Philemon and oversee the meeting in person but wasn't able to do so. Paul might have been a prisoner at this time, although the opening phrase (*"a prisoner of Jesus Christ"*) doesn't necessarily require that interpretation. At a minimum, Paul had ministry commitments that precluded him from being the escort. What the letter shows us is that Paul had confidence in the parties to come to restoration in light of his words and guidance in the matter.

APPLICATION FOR TODAY:

God values relationships. Is there a relationship you need to restore today?

58

HEBREWS 3:15-16

While it is said, Today if ye will hear his voice, harden not your hearts, as in the provocation. For some, when they had heard, did provoke: howbeit not all that came out of Egypt by Moses.

KEY MESSAGE:
FAITH IN GOD IS ESSENTIAL.

AS ONE WOULD EXPECT given the title of this book, the writer to the Hebrews uses many Old Testament examples. In chapter three, the author takes his audience back to Moses and the exodus from Egypt. He notes that a number of the Israelites hardened their hearts and didn't believe or trust in God. As a result, they didn't enter into the promised land and experience the joy of resting in God. Instead, they died in the wilderness. The author enjoins his readers to follow the example of the faithful ones who did trust God and followed Moses, rather than the doubters who died.

In Hebrews 3:7-11, the writer quotes from Psalm 95:7-11. Those verses are very familiar to me, as they're the "Venite" used in the Anglican Book of Common Prayer. I was raised in the Anglican Church, and for many years we would sing that psalm nearly every Sunday. It is, as the Latin word "venite" implies, part of the call to worship God.

In Hebrews 3, the author graphically describes the consequences of provoking the one true and holy God. In verse seventeen, the author notes that the result of doubt for the Israelites was that their "*carcasses fell in the wilderness.*" He notes that God swore that they would not enter into His rest due to their unbelief.

In Hebrews 4, the writer expands on this theme. He notes that we have a promise from God that we will enter into His rest as long as we trust, obey, and follow Him. He notes that merely hearing the gospel is not going to suffice—you need to receive it with faith and act upon it.

In conclusion, each of us needs to determine how we choose to receive the Word of God. Will you accept it and act upon it in faith so that you might receive the promised rest from God?

APPLICATION FOR TODAY:

Trust God and move forward in faith.

59

JAMES 3:16
For where envying and strife is, there is confusion and every evil work.

KEY MESSAGE:
EXAMINE YOUR MOTIVES AS YOU ACT.

THE BOOK OF JAMES is one of my favourites. He is eminently practical in his teaching. Some have protested that James appears to teach a "salvation by works" theology, but that is not the case. Rather, as we saw in Hebrews, if we have true faith in God, it should move us to act accordingly. As James says in 2:20b, *"faith without works is dead."*

In chapter three, James gives instruction about conduct that Christians need to avoid. He begins by addressing the words we say to others. In verse eight, he stresses that, if used improperly, our words can be *"an unruly evil, full of deadly poison."* In this era of social media and instant communication, I expect many of us can understand this assessment. Hardly a day goes by without a news article about someone's offensive comment on Twitter or some other platform. It's very easy to fire off words in anger but completely impossible to delete them later. (If this comment strikes home with you, I recommend the book *Before You Hit Send* by Emmerson Eggerichs.)

James later addresses the root cause of these bitter words: the attitude within our heart. When we envy others and allow strife to take hold in our hearts, we will have *"confusion and every evil work."* If our hearts are pure and right with God, our words will reflect that attitude, and we'll display a true Christian character.

In the closing verses of chapter three, James tells us the result of having a godly attitude. We will invite God's wisdom to flow through us, and the result will be conduct that is pure, peaceable, gentle, full of mercy and good fruits. It's easy to see that those results will cause others to ask what sets us apart from the conduct they see all around them, and it will open doors for the gospel. If that occurs, we need to continue to display Christlike character and proclaim God's love to all. James reminds us of this in chapter four, when he returns to discussing wrong attitudes and reminds us that we need to submit ourselves to God: *"Resist the devil and he will flee from you"* (James 4:7b).

APPLICATION FOR TODAY:
We need to examine our hearts and ensure that our attitude aligns with Jesus.

60

1 PETER 3:16

Having a good conscience; that, whereas they speak evil of you, as of evildoers, they may be ashamed that falsely accuse your good conversation in Christ.

KEY MESSAGE:
CONTINUE TO BE FAITHFUL IN DOING GOOD, EVEN IF YOU SUFFER AS A RESULT.

FIRST PETER 3 COULD be summarized as follows: you cannot argue someone into accepting Christ, but you might win them in by your good example. In verses one through six, he discusses how wives can win their husbands to the Lord. In verse seven, he gives a short admonition to husbands: honour your wife, or your prayers to God will be hindered. Peter then moves on to general recommendations for all of us. Verses eight through seventeen are replete with adjectives that should be used to describe followers of Christ: compassionate, courteous, seekers of peace, righteous. First Peter 3:15 is often quoted: *"But sanctify the Lord God in your hearts: and be ready always to give an answer to every man that asketh you a reason of the hope that is in you with meekness and fear."* In order for someone to ask you for the reason for your hope, you need to display an attitude of hope. It's been sad that during the COVID pandemic, many Christians seemed to be as fearful and depressed as non-Christians. We of all people should be able to display hope, for we know how the story ends and that this world is not our final home.

It's instructive that Peter doesn't promise that all will be smooth sailing in our daily lives. In fact, he "bookends" our subject verse with verses that inform us that we might endure hardship and suffering as Christians. In verse fourteen he says: "*But and if ye suffer for righteousness' sake, happy are ye: and be not afraid of their terror, neither be troubled.*" In verse seventeen, he adds this: "*For it is better, if the will of God be so, that ye suffer for well-doing than for evildoing.*" The message is clear: even if others don't understand us, even if others mock and persecute us, our attitude is to remain the same. Keep your conversation, deeds, and attitude positive and Christlike so that our accusers may be ashamed of their false accusations.

This is good instruction for our lives. When I was an active, practising lawyer, I had one boss who was terrified that a client might sue her or report her to the Law Society. I told her that I never worried about that or prayed about it. I told her that what I did pray was: "Lord, please do not let me be rightfully sued." In other words, I never wanted a client to have a legitimate basis to sue me or complain to the Law Society. We can't stop someone from accusing us, and we will meet some people who are never satisfied or happy. But our role as Christians is to have a good conscience, speak well and faithfully in Christ, and leave the consequences to God.

APPLICATION FOR TODAY:

Examine your own conduct and words. Do you meet the standard of 1 Peter 3:16?

61

2 PETER 3:16

As also in all his [Paul's] epistles, speaking in them of these things; in which are some things hard to be understood, which they that are unlearned and unstable wrest, as they do also the other scriptures, unto their own destruction.

KEY MESSAGE:
THE BEST COMMENTARY ON THE BIBLE IS THE BIBLE.

THIS IS AN IMPORTANT passage, because Peter endorses Paul as a *"beloved brother"* in verse fifteen. Paul was a late addition to the team of Christ followers. He'd been a dedicated persecutor of the followers of Jesus until Jesus Himself intervened in his life. Yet here Peter fully endorses Paul and his epistles. This is important for a number of reasons. Some critics of Christianity have made the false claim that the religion was really created, developed, and spread by Paul, even though he wasn't among the original twelve disciples, as much of the New Testament was written by him. Here Peter reveals that he has read at least some of Paul's epistles, and he agrees that they contain true Christian doctrine.

Secondly, Peter acknowledges that some aspects of Christian teaching can be hard to understand. The role of the believer is to seek to understand and apply the truths of Scripture, not to explain them away or argue against them. While it's common today to read or hear skeptics who don't want to accept the truth of the Bible, this verse shows that it's not a new phenomenon. In verse seventeen, Peter follows up on this theme and urges his readers to be wary and not be led astray from the true message of the gospel. On the contrary, as he says in verse eighteen (the final verse of this letter), we need to *"grow in grace and in the knowledge of our Lord and Saviour Jesus Christ."*

It's also worth noting that Peter and Paul didn't always see eye-to-eye in everything. In Galatians 2:11–15, Paul recounts a situation in which he rebuked Peter because Peter had withdrawn from fellowship with Gentile believers when some Jewish people arrived, fearing their opinion of him would be diminished. There are a couple of lessons for us in that illustration. First of all, we need to take heed when a fellow believer sees something that seems amiss in our behaviour. Our human reaction is probably to get our backs up and be upset, but it appears that Peter acknowledged that Paul had made a valid point. Secondly, we need to be alert to how fellow Christians are conducting themselves and not be too reluctant to gently suggest that they have strayed off course.

APPLICATION FOR TODAY:

All Scripture is endorsed by God, and we do well to persist in trying to follow it.

62

1 JOHN 3:16

Hereby perceive we the love of God, because he laid down his life for us: and we ought to pay down our lives for the brethren.

KEY MESSAGE:
FOLLOWING JESUS INVOLVES SACRIFICING YOURSELF.

THE FIRST LETTER OF John proclaims a clear message that can be summarized as follows: Jesus is fully God. Jesus has made us the children of God. God's children are to love just as Jesus loved us. Love involves sacrifice.

Chapter three opens with an often-quoted verse: *"Behold, what manner of love the Father hath bestowed upon us, that we should be called the sons of God: therefore the world knoweth us not because it knew him not."* The first part of this verse is more popular than the second part. Many of us know the chorus based on the first part. It appeals to our human nature to hear about receiving God's love and being called His child. It's not so appealing to hear that this means that the world won't know us and might even reject us. But this is part of John's message too. Following Jesus involves being willing to display God's relentless love to others, even in the face of persecution and rejection. Indeed, in verse thirteen, John sets out this simple message: *"Marvel not, my brethren, if the world hate you."* In verse fourteen, he declares that if we don't love our brother, we continue to *"abide in death."*

Following verse sixteen, John's instructions might remind us of the letter of James: God's love requires practical actions on our part. In verse seventeen, he simply asks this question: If we have abundant assets and see someone in need, how can we say that the love of God lives in us if we refuse to help him?

He expands on this message in verse eighteen when he directs us to not merely say that we love someone but to love *"in deed and in truth."*

John sums up his teaching in 3:23. We are to believe on the name of God's Son, Jesus Christ, and love one another, just as Jesus commanded us. He expands on this in chapters four and five. The word "love," or some variation of it (such as "beloved"), appears thirty-two times in these chapters. The closing verses of chapter four summarize what we have just read. John says that if we profess our love for God but hate our neighbour, then we are lying. He asks this simple question: If we don't love our brother, whom we have seen, how can we say we love God, whom we have not seen? He even answers his own question in the last verse of the chapter: God's commandment is that those who love God must also love their brother.

APPLICATION FOR TODAY:
Our Christian walk must display our love to those around us.

63

2 JOHN 1:13

JOHN'S SECOND LETTER IS a short letter. It consists of one chapter and is only thirteen verses in length. The final verse reads as follows:

> *The children of thy elect sister greet thee. Amen.*

KEY MESSAGE:
HOLD FAST TO GOD'S TRUTH, ESPECIALLY AMONG THOSE CLOSE TO YOU.

Much has been written about the recipient of this letter. Unlike 3 John, which we will come to next, this epistle doesn't identify the addressee by name. Verse one opens by telling us that the letter is written to *"the elect lady and her children."* This has caused some to speculate that the recipient wasn't an individual person but rather a church or body of believers. This theory ties in to the closing verse, quoted above. That verse would then refer to another body of believers, much in the way we might refer to a "sister church" today. John holds to this theme of a family and children. In verse four he says that he rejoiced greatly when he found that the elect lady's children were *"walking in truth."*

John continues to preach the message of love in this letter, but he tempers it with warnings about those who try to deceive believers. In verse seven, he says that there are many deceivers who don't believe that Jesus Christ came in the flesh. John pointedly declares that this false message *"is a deceiver and an antichrist."* He urges his reader to make this a firm line of doctrine. In fact, he says that if someone does not confess that Jesus came in the flesh, we should not receive that person into our house, nor bid them Godspeed. If the letter was indeed written to a church, then the message about not receiving someone into the house would, presumably, refer to their fellowship of believers.

APPLICATION FOR TODAY:
Show God's love to all, but do not tolerate false doctrine.

64

3 JOHN 1:14

JOHN'S THIRD LETTER IS also a short one. It consists of one chapter of fourteen verses. Verse fourteen reads as follows:

> *But I trust I shall shortly see thee, and we shall speak face to face. Peace be to thee. Our friends salute thee. Greet the friends by name.*

KEY MESSAGE:
HOLD FAST TO THE TRUTH.

This letter is addressed to an individual: *"the well-beloved Gaius"* (1:1). Beyond that, we don't have much information about him. The focus of this letter is to hold fast to the truth. In verses three and four, John says that he rejoiced greatly when he heard that Gaius was walking in the truth, and that he has no greater joy than to hear that his children walk in the truth. Near the end of the letter, John refers to a man named Demetrius and again says that he has a good report and walks in truth. By contrast, John mentions Diotrephes as being someone who seeks to have pre-eminence among people, who speaks malicious words and has embraced evil. While the references to specific individuals might seem irrelevant to us, the application is that we can't have ongoing fellowship with someone who claims to be a Christian but refuses to accept and embrace the true gospel message. It's vital to keep false doctrine out of our assemblies, lest it spread and infect others who might be new believers.

John also reminds Gaius to show love to the brethren and to strangers, showing hospitality to those whom he encounters. In this regard, John's third letter is reminiscent of his second one. In fact, verse thirteen of this letter is almost identical to verse twelve in the second letter. John notes that he had a lot to say to his addressees but will refrain from writing it down, as he hopes to soon see them in person.

Finally, one notes the importance of words and the value of blessing others. In verse two, John declares that he wishes above all things that Gaius might prosper and be in health, *"even as thy soul prospereth."* In verses five through seven, he commends Gaius for showing hospitality to others. Finally, in verse fourteen, he proclaims peace to his reader.

APPLICATION FOR TODAY:
Speak the truth in love and bless others with your words.

65

JUDE 1:16

JUDE'S LETTER IS ALSO only one chapter, but we do have a verse sixteen to consider. It reads as follows:

> *These are grumblers, complainers, walking according to their own lusts; and they mouth great swelling words, flattering people to gain advantage.*
> (NKJV)

KEY MESSAGE:
GOD WILL JUDGE THE UNGODLY.

Jude introduces himself as *"a bondservant of Jesus Christ, and brother of James"* (Jude 1, NKJV). This suggests that he was the half-brother of Jesus, one of those who did not believe in Jesus for much of His earthly ministry. See, however, a different explanation for this writer in the entry for Mark 3:16. Having come to faith in Christ, Jude wrote this brief epistle urging fellow believers to hold fast to their faith and be on guard against false believers, apostates, and evil people.

Jude refers to many Old Testament characters and stories in his letter: Sodom and Gomorrah (v. 7); Cain, Balaam, and the rebellion of Korah (v. 11); and Enoch (v. 14). He also makes reference to a non-biblical account of Michael contending with the devil for the body of Moses in verse nine. It seems to me that at least part of the reason for these references is to reassure his audience that Christianity was not a radical cult but rather the natural and logical conclusion of their Jewish faith.

The short summary of this letter could be the saying: "By their fruits you shall know them." We will encounter grumblers and complainers, whose only interest is serving their own needs. Such people may be different from those who actively promote false doctrine—the ones John warned his readers about in his letters. These *"spots in your love feast"* are *"serving only themselves"* (Jude 12, NKJV).

I recall a chance meeting with a woman whose family had been part of our congregation but had left. She candidly told me: "That church wasn't meeting our needs, so we left." I didn't admonish her but suggested that the point of a church congregation wasn't to meet the needs of those who attended but to minister to others. Jude urges his readers to allow God to judge and deal with these people in His perfect timing. His readers should dedicate themselves to their own pursuit of God. In verse twenty he urges them to build themselves up in their *"most holy faith"* and to pray in the Holy Spirit. He advises them to have discernment, for they will encounter some who need compassion, and others who need to be saved on an urgent basis, *"pulling them out of the fire"* (Jude 22–23).

There is a valuable message for us in these words. It's important not to be distracted by those who wish to sow confusion and pull us off track. We need to focus on Jesus and the work to which we've been called. We need to exercise discernment and make an assessment as to whether someone is actively working against the church, is in need of compassion, or is in need of an urgent rescue from sin and destruction. Then we need to act accordingly. In his closing benediction in verse twenty-four, Jude reminds us that Jesus is able to keep us from falling and to preserve us.

APPLICATION FOR TODAY:

Stay faithful and continue to work for the Lord.

66

REVELATION 3:16

So then because thou art lukewarm, and neither cold nor hot, I will spue thee out of my mouth.

KEY MESSAGE:
WORLDLY PROSPERITY IS NOT A SIGN OF SPIRITUAL MATURITY.

REVELATION 3:16 IS PART of John's record of God's letter to the church at Laodicea, one of the seven churches addressed in chapters two and three of the book. Laodicea was an extremely wealthy and self-satisfied city. It is therefore notable that, unlike the other churches, God does not have a word of commendation or approval for it. The letter to each church begins with God's declaration that *"I know thy works."* God sees and assesses all that we do. In most of the letters, God is able to find some redeeming quality in the church. Even in Sardis, where He says that the church has a reputation for being alive but is actually dead (3:1), God tempers this in verse four when He declares that there are still a few people there who have not defiled their garments and are worthy.

By contrast, the letter to Laodicea accuses it of being neither hot nor cold, merely lukewarm. Lukewarm water is pretty much useless; it's neither cold enough to refresh you nor hot enough for cooking or cleaning. In verse seventeen, John goes on to note that the church says it's rich and doesn't need anything, when in fact it's *"wretched, and miserable, and poor, and blind, and naked."* This is hardly an endorsement along the lines of "well done, thou good and faithful servant"!

These comments to the church would be particularly harsh if God saw it as beyond redemption, but that's not the case. In verse eighteen, He gives them counsel of what they need to do to change their ways. In verse nineteen, He reassures them that *"As many as I love, I rebuke and chasten."* God urges them to be zealous and to repent. Revelation 3:20 is often quoted as a verse of reassurance to us today: *"Behold, I stand at the door, and knock: if any man hear my voice, and open the door, I will come in to him, and will sup with him, and he with me."* God is a gentleman: He will not barge in uninvited. He is knocking at the door, and it's up to you to decide whether you wish to let Him into your heart and enjoy that fellowship, or if you're content to stay *"wretched and miserable."*

APPLICATION FOR TODAY:

Examine your heart and take stock of where you need to repent and become zealous.

PART TWO
DEVOTIONS FROM THE GOSPEL OF JOHN

KEY MESSAGE:

DURING HIS EARTHLY MINISTRY, Jesus declared that He was the Messiah, and many believed Him.

OVERVIEW

It has become fashionable in some circles today to say that Jesus was "merely a great prophet." Some people even make the preposterous claim that Jesus didn't see Himself as the Messiah or declare that He was the One. Such people have either not read the Gospel of John, or they have chosen not to believe what he wrote. As we will see, Jesus repeatedly said that He was the Messiah, and many people in His day recognized Him as such.

BACKGROUND

John was one of the twelve disciples. He was the author of the Gospel of John, the three epistles that bear his name, and the book of Revelation. As far as we know, he was the only one of the twelve disciples to live a long life and die a natural death. The name John is a popular name for saints. The *Penguin Dictionary of Saints* lists thirty-five entries for saints named John, beginning with the "apostle and evangelist." The author of that book notes that his entries only deal with the principal saints named John, as there are sixty-four saints by that name "in the Roman Martyrology alone."[5]

John was the brother of James the Greater, another one of the twelve disciples. I pause here to note that their lives show how God is the One in control of our lives, and He has the right to deal with us as He sees best. James was the first of the twelve put to a martyr's death. In Acts 12:2, we're told that King Herod "*killed James the brother of John with the sword.*" When the king saw that this pleased the Jews, he proceeded to take Peter as a prisoner—but God's angel released Peter from jail. In contrast to his brother,

---

[5] Attwater, 185.

who was the first disciple martyred, John lived until he died at an old age, apparently in Ephesus.

John also shows the power of Jesus to transform lives. James and John were called the "*sons of thunder*," so we can assume they had an impulsive side to them. However, they were chosen to see the Transfiguration of the Lord (along with Peter), and John's letters preach the message of love and gentleness.

APPLICATION FOR TODAY:

As John was an eyewitness to the life and ministry of Jesus, his words merit close attention.

68

JOHN 1

"In the beginning was the Word, and the Word was with God, and the Word was God" (John 1:1).

KEY MESSAGE:
JESUS WAS THE WORD FROM THE BEGINNING OF TIME, ONE WITH GOD.

MANY CHRISTIANS ARE FAMILIAR with this key message from the opening line of the song, "What a Beautiful Name" by Ben Fielding and Brooke Ligertwood. The key message is that Jesus always was God, from the beginning of time, and appeared in human form on earth. Even George Harrison recognized this when he wrote the song "Awaiting on You All," because he refers to the eternal nature of Jesus. It's not clear whether Harrison ever committed himself to Jesus—he seemed to want to adopt bits and pieces of various theologies—but in that song, he was on solid ground for most of the lyrics.

John 1 contains one of the most succinct distinctions between the old covenant and the new covenant. In verse seventeen, we read, *"For the law was given by Moses, but grace and truth came by Jesus Christ."* This chapter also contains some of the earliest declarations that Jesus was the Son of God. When Jesus came to John the Baptist to be baptized in the Jordan, John declared, *"Behold the Lamb of God, which taketh away the sin of the world"* (John 1:29b). This is followed with John's further profession, *"And I saw, and bare record that this is the Son of God"* (v. 34).

As chapter one continues, we see the first disciples coming to Jesus: Andrew, Simon Peter (Andrew's brother), Philip, and Nathanael. In John 1:49b, Nathanael declares, *"Rabbi, thou art the Son of God; thou art the King of*

Israel." Apart from this early and fervent declaration, not much is written about Nathanael, for he's not the subject of the New Testament. Scholars generally think that Nathanael is the same man referred to as Bartholomew by the other writers of Gospels, but even they don't have much to say about him. The *Penguin Dictionary of Saints* has this to say: "Except that he was called to be one of the twelve apostles, nothing certain is known about him; but it is possible that he is the same man as Nathanael."[6] What we take from his declaration is that those who actually walked with Jesus and knew Him best certainly understood that He was the long-awaited Messiah. He wasn't merely another prophet or just a good teacher.

APPLICATION FOR TODAY:
Jesus is the Lamb who has taken away the sins of the world.

---

[6] Ibid., 55.

69

JOHN 2

"And his disciples remembered that it was written, The zeal of thine house hath eaten me up" (John 2:17).

KEY MESSAGE:
JESUS TAKES CHARGE AND SHOWS HIS AUTHORITY

IN CHAPTER TWO, JOHN recounts two principal events that, at first glance, don't seem to be connected. Upon closer inspection, however, the connection emerges: Jesus had authority over nature and humanity. He wasn't merely a prophet or a teacher.

In John 2:1–11, John tells us about the wedding in Cana of Galilee, attended by Jesus; His mother, Mary; and His disciples. This is the *"beginning of miracles,"* which *"manifested forth his glory; and his disciples believed on him"* (v. 11). The miracle, of course, was the transformation of water into wine, and not merely wine, but the best wine offered at the marriage feast.

Mary clearly knew that her Son was capable of performing this miracle, as she was the one who told Jesus that there was no wine available. She wasn't merely making conversation or complaining: she was confident that Jesus could remedy the problem. We can take several lessons from this incident. First, Jesus cares about our frail human needs, for He provided the best wine for a wedding feast. He didn't spurn the request from Mary or say that it wasn't important enough for His attention. Secondly, Jesus declared that He had authority over all things, including the elements of nature. He transformed water into wine; that wine never existed in the form of grapes. Finally, Jesus didn't make an ostentatious display of His power, for verse nine tells us that the ruler of the feast didn't even know how the wine had appeared. Jesus isn't some sort of cosmic magician who called the crowd together and waved a magic wand so those present would fawn over Him.

In John 2:12–25, John describes Jesus clearing the temple area of those who had turned it into an early shopping mall. Again, Jesus showed His authority—this time over men and beasts (the sheep and oxen mentioned in verse fifteen). Obviously, the merchants in that area outnumbered Jesus, but He prevailed. We aren't told that they offered much resistance to Him, despite the fact that they should have been able to eject Jesus from their midst. It's possible that the merchants knew Jesus was correct and that they shouldn't be doing business in the Temple area. It's also possible that they simply noticed how Jesus acted with conviction and took authority over them and the situation. Some have tried to suggest that the traders were overwhelmed by the raging appearance of a wild man attacking them, but such speculation isn't based upon the Scripture.

Nowhere in this account does John describe Jesus as angry, raging, or out of control. On the contrary, Jesus first observed the situation, then took the time to make a scourge of small cords, and then set about clearing the area. His words to the assembly at least implied the source of His authority, as He referred to "*my Father's house*" (v. 16).

In verse seventeen, John indicates that this incident was a fulfillment of Psalm 69:9, which says that "*the zeal of thine house hath eaten me up.*" Some of those present asked Jesus for a sign of His authority. His reply, which they didn't understand, was a prediction of His death and resurrection: "Destroy this temple, and in three days I will raise it up" (v. 19b). Those in attendance took Him to be describing the earthly temple He had just cleared; in fact, as we are told in verse twenty-one, Jesus was speaking about His own body.

APPLICATION FOR TODAY:

Jesus remains the same. He is Lord over all things.

70

JOHN 3

"Jesus answered and said unto him [Nicodemus], Verily, verily, I say unto thee, Except a man be born again, he cannot enter into the kingdom of God" (John 3:3).

KEY MESSAGE:
TWO PARALLEL STATEMENTS ABOUT THE NEED FOR SALVATION—AND HOW TO GET THERE.

JOHN 3 IS PROBABLY best known for Nicodemus' visit to Jesus, and for the much-loved verse sixteen. While I will touch on those portions here, I want to focus on two other sections of the chapter. The two longest speeches in this chapter are given by Jesus in His answer to Nicodemus, and by John the Baptist in the last half of the chapter.

After Jesus provides a response to Nicodemus' question about being born again (v. 4), Nicodemus poses a follow up question: *"How can these things be?"* (v. 9b). Nicodemus was puzzled by his spiritual discussion with Jesus, yet he wasn't an uneducated peasant or the typical man-on-the-street. John 3:1 describes him as a Pharisee and *"a ruler of the Jews."* In response to the question in verse nine, Jesus takes the floor and speaks from verse ten through to verse twenty-one. This passage includes the famous verse sixteen: *"For God so loved the world, that he gave his only begotten Son, that whosoever believeth in him should not perish, but have everlasting life."*

The following verses are equally important. In verse seventeen, Jesus stresses the need to make a personal commitment to Him in order to be saved. In verse eighteen, we find the first of our two parallel statements about salvation. Jesus says that if you don't believe in Him, you're condemned already, because you have *"not believed in the name of the only begotten Son of God."* Clearly Jesus is saying that He's the Son of God and the way to salvation. Nowhere in this chapter does Jesus say that He's a teacher, rabbi, or prophet. In fact, these terms are used by Nicodemus in verse two, and Jesus spends most of the rest of their discussion correcting this assessment.

We're not told here of Nicodemus' reaction to his meeting with Jesus. We learn in John 19:39 that Nicodemus provided the spices for the burial of Jesus. While this indicates that Nicodemus was a kind man who continued to respect Jesus, it doesn't inform us of whether he actually understood and accepted Jesus as Saviour and Lord.

After the conclusion of Jesus' words to Nicodemus, John simply turns the page and moves on to another scene. In John 3:22 Jesus and his disciples go to Judea, and Jesus baptizes people there. In the next verse, the scene shifts to John the Baptist, because he was also performing baptisms in that location. Some of John's disciples and some of the Jews inform John the Baptist that Jesus is also baptizing people and that *"all men come to him"* (v. 26). If they were hoping to provoke some sign of jealousy in John, they were sadly disappointed. On the contrary, John the Baptist informs them all that this is precisely what is supposed to happen. He explains that Jesus is from heaven and is above all (v. 31), while John is merely from earth. The chapter ends with the second of our parallel declarations (vv. 35–36). John declares that Jesus is the Son of God and that if we believe on the Son of God, we have eternal life, while *"he that believeth not on the Son shall not see life; but the wrath of God abideth on him"* (v. 36).

This chapter is a valuable response to those who want to call Jesus a good teacher, because that's how Nicodemus began his comments: *"we know thou art a teacher come from God"* (v. 2). He wasn't the only religious leader who recognized something special and valuable in Jesus. However, both Jesus and John the Baptist spend most of this chapter explaining that Jesus isn't merely a teacher sent from God: He is God, and He alone offers us the way to be saved instead of being condemned.

APPLICATION FOR TODAY:
Jesus remains the only way to salvation!

71

JOHN 4:1–42

"The woman said unto him, I know that Messiah cometh, which is called Christ: when he is come, he will tell us all things. Jesus said unto her, I that speak to thee am he"
(John 4:25–26).

KEY MESSAGE:
NO ONE IS BEYOND THE LOVE OF GOD.

THIS PORTION OF JOHN 4 is the story of the Samaritan woman at the well. While this woman was Jesus' point of entry to the town where she lived, the entire passage shows Jesus doing something the Jews did not do: spend time with Samaritans: "… *the Jews have no dealings with the Samaritans*" (John 4:9). Indeed, one can see a mild form of the Jews' views on Samaritans in Jesus' comment to the woman in John 4:22: "*Ye worship ye know not what: we know what we worship: for salvation is of the Jews.*"

God breaks down many prejudices and cultural barriers in this passage. John says that Jesus needs to go through Samaria to get to His ultimate destination (v.4), but in practice, the Jewish people would travel great distances out of their way to circumnavigate that nation. Secondly, Jesus initiates conversation with the woman who came to the well, which is something no normal Jewish man would do. Jesus knows her background and that she's a social outcast. We can glean that fact because the woman came to the well during the heat of mid-day, or the sixth hour (v. 6). She came when she knew that no one from her city would be at the well. Thirdly, when the rest of the city asks Jesus to stay with them (v. 40), He stays for two full days. Clearly, He must have stayed with someone from the city, although the Bible doesn't inform us of who that was.

In her initial conversation with Jesus, the woman is prepared to call Him "*a prophet*" (v. 19), largely based on the Lord's comment that He knows she's been married five times and is now living with someone who isn't her husband. In verse twenty-six, Jesus directly proclaims to the woman that He is the promised Messiah.

There is no equivocation or need for inferences in His direct declaration. Immediately after this encounter, this social outcast goes to the city, initiates discussion with the men of the town, and brings them to see Jesus. She declares to them that Jesus is the Christ. It's somewhat remarkable that the men immediately come to see for themselves rather than rejecting her words out of hand due to her background. It's possible that they might have been engaging in some measure of trying to save face.

After Jesus is with them for the two days, they tell the woman that they accept Him as the Messiah "*not because of thy saying: for we have heard him ourselves ...*" (v. 42). In any event, Jesus leaves that city with many more who believe in Him as Messiah—all of whom would be considered unclean by the Jews.

APPLICATION FOR TODAY:

Take the time to speak with people. You never know who might accept Jesus!

72

JOHN 4:43-54

"This is again the second miracle that Jesus did, when he was come out of Judea into Galilee"
(John 4:54).

KEY MESSAGE:

THE WORD OF JESUS HAS THE POWER TO HEAL—EVEN AT A DISTANCE.

THE SECOND PORTION OF John 4 recounts Jesus' journey to Galilee, specifically to the city of Cana, where Jesus had performed the first miracle of turning the water into wine. In Cana, a *"certain nobleman"* (v. 46) approached Jesus because the man's son was sick and he was seeking Jesus' healing power. John tells us that the ill son wasn't in Cana but rather at Capernaum, another city in Galilee. In a day of limited transportation options, this was a journey of some distance. It's possible that the nobleman had some means of transportation, but the Gospel doesn't provide that information. Instead, we're told that the nobleman initially asked Jesus to travel to Capernaum to heal his son.

Jesus' reply is interesting: *"Except ye see signs and wonders, ye will not believe"* (v. 48b). I find this a little curious, since it seems to me that the nobleman coming to Jesus means that he did believe already. There didn't appear to be any doubt in the man's mind that Jesus could heal his son, for he didn't preface his request with "if you can" or "if you will." In any event, Jesus' reply resulted in the man making a more urgent plea: *"Sir, come down ere my child die"* (v. 49).

But Jesus did not "come down" to Capernaum. On the contrary, He simply said, *"Go thy way; thy son liveth"* (v. 50a). John tells us that the nobleman immediately believed the words of Jesus and went on his way. John then completes the story by telling us that as the nobleman headed home, his servants met him and told him that his son had been healed. In verse fifty-three, John notes that the healing occurred "*at the same hour*" as when Jesus spoke the words of healing. We also obtain some indication of the distance between Cana and Capernaum, because the servants tell their master that the son was healed "*Yesterday at the seventh hour*" (v. 52). This means that it was more than a day's journey between the two cities.

We sometimes say that there is no distance in prayer. This brief gospel story is a vivid illustration of that truth. While it's wonderful to be able to pray with someone in person, there is no need to be physically present in the same place to experience the power of God. Given the current pandemic, many of our prayers have taken place by the modern blessing of systems such as Zoom. While we should be grateful for opportunities to gather and pray together in person, do not be reluctant to expect that God can do great miracles at any distance.

APPLICATION FOR TODAY:
There is no distance too great for Jesus to bridge with His power!

73

JOHN 5:1–18

"Therefore the Jews sought the more to kill him [Jesus], because he not only had broken the sabbath, but had said also that God was his Father, making himself equal with God" (John 5:18).

KEY MESSAGE:
JESUS DECLARES THAT HE IS GOD, AND HIS WORKS SUPPORT HIS CLAIM.

THE FIRST SECTION OF John 5 records another miraculous healing by Jesus. This one takes place at the pool of Bethesda. John sets the stage by telling us that this pool had one unique attribute. At certain times, an angel would stir up the water, and the first person to enter the pool afterwards would be healed of any infirmity. There are a number of interesting aspects to this story. Jesus came to the place, assessed the situation, and—as far as we're told—only healed one man. We aren't told why this was the case. It's possible that none of the other ill people in attendance had faith in Jesus. One would think that having seen a lame man healed, others would come forward and ask Jesus to heal them too. But that's my own sidebar to the story. It's also possible that we have the answer in verse thirteen, where we learn that Jesus had already *"conveyed himself away"* shortly after healing the lame man.

What we do know is that Jesus encountered a man who had been lame for thirty-eight years (v.5). Jesus approached the man and asked him a simple question: "Will you be made whole?" Interestingly, the man didn't answer the question. Instead, he gave an excuse as to why he wasn't already whole: *"Sir, I have no man, when the water is troubled, to put me into the pool: but while I am coming, another steppeth down before me*" (v. 7b). Again, my mind reels with questions. Did the man live at the pool day and night? If so, did someone bring food to him? Did he live somewhere else and have friends or relatives bring him to the pool each day? In either case, why were his helpers willing to do this task each day but not to wait around to help the man into the pool? Instead, they repeated their routine every day—for thirty-eight years! Jesus cuts through the excuses: *"Rise, take up thy bed, and walk."* Immediately the man was healed, picked up his mat, and walked (vv. 8–9).

As was often the case, the religious leaders weren't happy for the man or his miraculous healing. On the contrary, they were angry that Jesus had the nerve to "do work" (healing) on the Sabbath, and that He told the man to carry his bed, which also qualified as work in their minds. At that point, the man couldn't identify Jesus, since He had already left the scene. But that's not the end of the story. John informs us that Jesus subsequently found the man in the temple. Perhaps the man was thanking God for his miraculous healing. Jesus then completed the picture by telling the man not to sin any more, or something worse could come upon him (v. 14).

This exchange enabled the man to tell the religious leaders that Jesus had been his healer. When they complained to Jesus that He'd been working on the Sabbath, Jesus simply replied: *"My Father has been working until now, and I have been working"* (v. 17, NKJV). This further enraged the religious leaders to the point of wanting to kill Jesus.

Let's summarize what Jesus did to enrage them. First, He healed a man on the Sabbath. Second, He told the man to do work (carry his bed) on the Sabbath. Third, He told the man to avoid sinning—thus implying that Jesus had power over the forgiveness of sins. Fourth, He said that He was equal to God the Father. The religious leaders either didn't want to ask the question or didn't care about the answer: "Is this man uttering blasphemy, or is he telling us the truth—that He is God?"

APPLICATION FOR TODAY:

What is your conclusion? Is Jesus the Son of God, or is He a man uttering blasphemy?

74

JOHN 5:19-47

Jesus said: *"Most assuredly, I say to you, he who hears My word and believes in Him who sent Me has everlasting life, and shall not come into judgment, but has passed from death into life"* (John 5:24, NKJV).

KEY MESSAGE:
JESUS IS GOD AND IS THE ONLY WAY FOR US TO REACH SALVATION.

APART FROM THE OPENING words of John 5:19 (*"Then Jesus answered and said unto them"*), this entire passage consists of Jesus speaking to the religious leaders of the day. It constitutes a lecture, or possibly a sermon, to the people there. In his address, Jesus emphasizes the Father and the Son. The word "Father" appears thirteen times; the word "Son" is found on nine occasions. These are in addition to references to "God" or the personal pronoun, "I."

Jesus' message is explicit and clear: God the Father and I are one. There is only one way to be saved; if you don't believe in me, then you're already condemned. Along the way, Jesus has some pointed words for the religious leaders. He says that the Father has sent Him to them, but that they *"have neither heard His voice at any time, nor seen his form. But you do not have His word abiding in you, because whom he sent, Him you do not believe"* (5:37–38, NKJV). In verse forty-two, Jesus says that He knows that they don't have the love of God in them. This seems quite apt, given that this passage immediately follows their reaction to the healing of the lame man.

Jesus also refers to John the Baptist and to Moses. He says that the leaders heard from John and appreciated his ministry but didn't accept that he was the forerunner to Jesus. He concludes His message by saying that the leaders claim to trust in Moses, but that they don't really do so. Jesus says that if they truly believed in Moses, they would accept Jesus, because Moses was writing about Jesus.

One cannot fail to understand the message of Jesus in this passage. To paraphrase C.S. Lewis, this sermon alone shows that Jesus can't be taken for just a prophet or a good teacher. He is either the Messiah, the one and only route to salvation, or He's a complete lunatic. Each of us needs to read His words carefully and decide which option to choose. Please understand that the choice is literally a matter of where you will spend eternity. As our highlighted verse says, accepting Jesus will lead to everlasting life.

While we can assume that the religious leaders weren't impressed or persuaded by this address, John doesn't spend any time informing us of their reaction. Instead, as we will see in chapter six, he informs us that Jesus then went across the Sea of Galilee. Therefore, the words of Jesus weren't just directed at the religious leaders of the day, but rather to everyone for all time.

APPLICATION FOR TODAY:

What is your decision? Is Jesus your Saviour?

75

JOHN 6:1–34

Then Jesus said to them, "Most assuredly, I say to you, Moses did not give you the bread from heaven, but My Father gives you the true bread from heaven. For the bread of God is He who comes down from heaven and gives life to the world." (John 6:32–33, NKJV)

KEY MESSAGE:
JESUS IS THE TRUE BREAD OF LIFE.

JOHN 6 IS LONG (seventy-one verses) and rich, with familiar miracles and teaching. In this first section, we find two miracles: Jesus feeding the multitude with five loaves and two fish, and Jesus walking on the water. We also see a significant disconnect between the crowd's expectations and desires and what Jesus wished to communicate. We also see the fickle nature of the people.

After Jesus fed the crowd of about five thousand with the food from a young lad, Jesus perceived that the crowd wanted to take Him and make Him a king by force. But Jesus wasn't on earth to make an earthly kingdom, nor to be their miracle-worker. So He left them and went up to a mountain alone. Jesus subsequently joined His disciples in their boat after walking out to them on the Sea of Tiberias (Galilee). When the crowd managed to arrive the next day, you can practically hear their mental wheels spinning in 6:22–25. They know that Jesus didn't get into the boat with His disciples, and they can see that there's no other boat there, yet Jesus is there. They ask Him when He arrived, but one suspects that their real question would have been: "How on earth did He get over here?" If they thought it through, it might have led them to the realization that another miracle had occurred. Instead, Jesus chose not to answer their question, instead analyzing their motives and urging them to strive for the true meat that leads to everlasting life.

In John 6:28, the people ask Jesus a question that many continue to ask today: *"What shall we do, that we may work the works of God?"* (NKJV). In other words: "How do I earn my way into heaven?" Jesus' answer is essential and is one reason why the Christian faith is unique. Jesus doesn't give a list of things to do to earn our way into heaven and win God's approval. Instead, He tells them simply: *"This is the work of God, that you believe on him whom he hath sent"* (v. 29, NKJV).

Faith in Jesus is the way to eternal life. The response of the people is extraordinary. Having seen the miracle of the loaves and fish, and having at least the evidence of another miracle in Jesus' crossing of the sea without a boat, the people ask Him to show them a sign so that they might believe in Him! Again, Jesus points them back to His previous answer: Moses didn't give you bread from heaven [My Father did that]. Now you need to believe in the True Bread from heaven [Me]. The people were still thinking in worldly terms and about what they needed to do. In the balance of chapter six, Jesus continues to try to get the message across to the people. The result was that *"from that time many of his disciples went back, and walked no more with him"* (v. 66, NKJV).

APPLICATION FOR TODAY:

Are you still trying to do something to earn God's favour, or are you firm in your faith in Jesus?

76

JOHN 6:35-71

[Jesus said] I am the living bread which came down from heaven: if any man eat of this bread, he shall live forever: and the bread that I will give is my flesh, which I will give for the life of the world.
(John 6:51)

KEY MESSAGE:
JESUS' PERFECT SACRIFICE GIVES US SALVATION.

IN THIS SECTION OF John 6, Jesus repeats His statement that He is the bread of life. He also predicts—albeit somewhat cryptically—His crucifixion, resurrection, and eventual ascension back into heaven. While we're able to read these words from the viewpoint of understanding their eventual fulfillment, it's no wonder His audience at the time were bewildered and even offended by what they heard. However, one could not miss the importance of Jesus' statements that began with "I am." Yahweh is the great "I AM," as the Lord told Moses in the wilderness. As a result, the Jewish religious leaders were extremely sensitive to anyone who used that phrase in a way that could be considered blasphemous. Let's look at the words of Jesus with that background and context.

In John 6:35, Jesus says, *"I am the bread of life."* Lest there be any ambiguity in those words, He continues by saying that *"he that cometh to Me shall never hunger; and he that believeth on Me shall never thirst."* This can only be taken as a statement of His divinity. In verse forty-eight, He repeats: *"I am that bread of life."* In verse fifty-one, as quoted above, Jesus says that He is *"the bread which cometh down from heaven."* In verse fifty-eight, He refers to Himself as *"that bread which came down from heaven."*

Jesus also states several times that He came down from heaven (vv. 38, 50, 51, 58) and that He was sent by the Father (vv. 32, 37, 39, 40, 44, 57). These words are very clear. While we understand the words about eating His flesh and drinking His blood today due to the context of the Last Supper and the ongoing ordinance of communion, it's not surprising that the audience at the time was confused and even offended by these words. As recorded in verse fifty-two, Jesus' audience debated among themselves, asking the fair question: *"How can this man give us his flesh to eat?"* In verse sixty, we're told that even many of Jesus' disciples called this a *"hard saying"* and asked who could understand it.

Jesus also spoke prophetically about His crucifixion when he said that He would give His life for the world (v. 51) and that His death and resurrection would mean that those who believe in Him would live forever (vv. 53–58). Finally, in verse sixty-two, He speaks of His ascension and return to heaven.

In summary, many of His former disciples turned away at this point. The twelve apostles, and likely some others, remained loyal. Peter spoke for that group when he said that Jesus had the words of eternal life and that *"we have come to believe and know that You are the Christ, the Son of the living God"* (v. 69, NKJV). In response, Jesus made a reference to the fact that one of them would nonetheless betray Him.

APPLICATION FOR TODAY:

Jesus is still the true bread who came from heaven. His words are life!

7

JOHN 7

"In the last day, that great day of the feast, Jesus stood and cried, saying, If any man thirst, let him come unto me, and drink" (John 7:37).

KEY MESSAGE:
GOD'S TIMING IS SOVEREIGN.

MOST OF JOHN 7 takes place during the Jewish Feast of Tabernacles. There are two themes running through this chapter. The first one is God's timing. The second one is the division among the people and the religious leaders as to whether or not Jesus was the Messiah.

God's timing is sovereign and essential. Jesus was to die for the sins of the world, but only when God's appointed time had fully come. The chapter starts with a discussion between Jesus and His half-brothers. At that time, they didn't believe in Him, but we know that some of them later came to faith and grew into leaders in the early church. In verses three through five, Jesus' brothers urge Him to go to the Feast of Tabernacles. I infer that they expected Him to fall flat on His face, and then this silly notion of being a prophet could be put to rest.

Jesus replies to them in John 7:6: *"My time is not yet come: but your time is alway ready."* Later, in verse ten, Jesus eventually goes to the feast, *"not openly, but as it were in secret."* John doesn't provide any additional details about how Jesus went in secret. Did He travel without His disciples? Did He somehow change His appearance? In verse fourteen, however, Jesus reveals Himself and begins teaching.

The next reference to timing comes in verse thirty. The religious leaders reject Jesus and want to arrest Him, but John says: *"no man laid hands on him, because his hour was not yet come."* Finally, in John 7:44–46, the chief priests and Pharisees send officers to arrest Jesus, but they return empty-handed. When the religious leaders demand an explanation for this failure, the officers simply reply, "*Never man spake like this man*" (v. 46). The entire episode ends in verse fifty-three, with every man simply going home. (In John 8:20, John again informs us that no one was able to lay hands on Jesus to arrest Him, "*for his hour had not yet come.*")

The second theme running through this chapter is the division among the people about whether Jesus could be the Messiah. As noted above, His half-brothers did not believe in Him. In John 7:12, we see two main opinions: some said Jesus was "a good man" and some said "no, he is deceiving people." When Jesus began teaching, some of the people grudgingly admitted that He knew what He was talking about, but they were at a loss to explain this, given His lack of formal education (7:15). In verses twenty-six and twenty-seven, the people openly question whether Jesus could be "*the very Christ.*" This discussion intensifies in verse thirty-one, with many of the people asking whether it would be possible for Christ to do any more miracles than Jesus has already performed. The debate continues in verses forty and forty-one, with some calling Jesus the Christ, and some calling Him a prophet.

Two main objections are raised to the idea of Jesus being the Messiah, and both of them are odd. The first one is the belief that Jesus came from Galilee, as they knew the prophecy that the Messiah was to be born in Bethlehem. It has long seemed curious to me that no one thought to ask Jesus (or even His half-brothers) where He had been born. Perhaps this is one of those popular misconceptions that people don't investigate because they're so certain that they already know the answer.

The second objection is raised by the religious leaders, and it's really one of pride. In John 7:48–49, the leaders arrogantly state that none of them has believed in Jesus, so why would any of the people believe in Him? They even go so far as to say that the people who follow Jesus are "*cursed*" (v. 49). The sole cautionary word among the leaders comes from Nicodemus, the one who visited Jesus in John 3. He urges his fellow leaders to listen to Jesus and know exactly what He's doing. This doesn't lead to any great resolution. On the contrary, the rest of the leaders fall back on the objection raised above: this man is from Galilee, and no prophet comes from there! This strikes me as a variation of "because I said so!" In any event, the chapter doesn't end with any sign of agreement among the people. Each of them seems to hold to his own opinion.

APPLICATION FOR TODAY:
What opinion do you hold on to despite the evidence God is providing?

78

JOHN 8:1–13

"Then Jesus spoke to them again, saying, 'I am the light of the world. He who follows Me shall not walk in darkness, but have the light of life'"
(John 8:12, NKJV).

KEY MESSAGE:
JESUS OFFERS FORGIVENESS OF SINS BUT DOES ASK THAT WE TURN AWAY FROM SIN.

THE FIRST PORTION OF John 8 presents a familiar story of a woman who was taken in the act of adultery (v. 4) and brought to Jesus by the religious leaders. As the story unfolds, it's clear that the religious leaders aren't seeking justice or mercy; they're seeking to trap Jesus—and they fail. One wonders whether the entire situation was manufactured, as it's hard to imagine how the religious leaders could just happen to find a woman engaging in adultery.

When they bring her to Jesus, they say that Moses commanded that such sinners should be stoned to death. While this is true, it's not the entire truth, and the Pharisees certainly knew the full extent of the Old Testament law. The law, as set out in Deuteronomy 22:22, required that both of the participants were to die. The fact that the Pharisees only presented the woman to Jesus shows a selective decision on their part. Interestingly, Jesus doesn't point out this anomaly, as it's not germane to the lesson He plans to teach them. Instead, after spending a few moments writing in the dirt, "*as though He heard them not*" (v. 6), Jesus gives the sage answer: "*He that is without sin among you, let him first cast a stone at her*" (v. 7). Jesus then resumes writing on the ground until all of the accusers have left, "*being convicted by their own conscience*" (v. 9).

Jesus then stands up and turns His attention to the woman, who is still before Him. While He knows the answer to the question, Jesus nonetheless asks her what happened to her accusers. Is there not one left? She replies that none of them is left. Jesus then informs her that He also is not condemning her, but He tells her to *"go and sin no more"* (v. 11). This is an important part of this account! Jesus doesn't condemn us, but if we truly come to Him, He does ask that we go and sin no more! Forgiveness of sins and freedom in Jesus should never lead to a licence to live a sinful life.

Having dispensed perfect grace and perfect justice, Jesus says the words highlighted at the start of this section. Again, we see the phrase "I am," which is a clear reference to His assertion of divinity. He also promises that those who follow Him will not be walking in darkness but will have the light of life. The Pharisees, of course, don't accept this declaration. What follows is a long discussion between Jesus and the Pharisees.

APPLICATION FOR TODAY:
Jesus forgives us our sins and calls us into a holy life.

79

JOHN 8:14–59

"Jesus said to them, 'Most assuredly, I say to you, before Abraham was, I AM'"
(John 8:58, NKJV).

KEY MESSAGE:

THE PHARISEES CALLED THEMSELVES "ABRAHAM'S CHILDREN," BUT JESUS WAS THE ONE WHO ACTUALLY KNEW ABRAHAM!

THIS PASSAGE IS ONE of the longest exchanges between Jesus and the Pharisees. While Jesus speaks clearly and consistently about Himself and God the Father, the Pharisees either don't understand or don't want to accept that Jesus is the Son of God. In some of their earlier exchanges with Jesus, the Pharisees invoked the name or authority of Moses. In this passage, they refer to Abraham. Along the way, Jesus makes oblique references to His crucifixion, *"when you lift up the Son of Man"* (v. 28, NKJV), and to His ascension, *"I am not of this world"* (v. 23, NKJV). While we can readily appreciate that the Pharisees didn't understand these allusions, many of Jesus' other comments are clear to those who are willing to hear them.

In John 8:14–30, Jesus repeatedly says that the Father sent Him to them, and that if they had truly known the Father, they would know Jesus. He explains that He is doing the work of the Father. John tells us that as Jesus spoke these words, *"many believed in Him"* (John 8:30, NKJV). The Pharisees, of course, were not persuaded. When Jesus says that His disciples will know the truth and the truth will set them free (v. 32), the Pharisees invoke the name of Abraham. They declare that they are Abraham's descendants and have never been in bondage, so they don't need anyone to set them free. In His long reply (vv. 34–47), Jesus says that in reality they are the children of the devil because they don't listen to God's words and are seeking to kill His Son. Jesus notes that the devil is a liar and a murderer and is not interested in truth or the One who speaks the truth.

This passage reaches its climax in verses forty-eight through fifty-nine. Jesus promises eternal life to His followers, and the Pharisees scoff at this declaration. They say that Abraham is dead, and the prophets are dead, so who does Jesus think He is? Jesus responds that the Pharisees say that the Father is their God, but they have not known Him. He adds that if He said He didn't know the Father, then He would be a liar as they are. Jesus concludes this address by saying that Abraham *"rejoiced to see My day, and he saw it and was glad"* (v. 56, NKJV).

The Pharisees retort that Jesus is not even fifty years old, so how could He possibly have seen Abraham? This brings us to our highlighted verse. Jesus makes a clear and unequivocal declaration that He is God: *"Before Abraham was, I AM."* In response, the Pharisees take up stones, intending to stone Jesus. John then states—in rather understated fashion—that Jesus *"hid Himself and went out of the temple, going through the midst of them, and so passed by"* (v. 59, NKJV). I'm not sure what one can make of this other than that Jesus either cloaked Himself with invisibility or, at a minimum, became invisible to the Pharisees. I don't see how else one can interpret the fact that Jesus was able to pass through the midst of them without observation. John doesn't dwell on this point, however, as he is moving forward to chapter nine and another miraculous healing.

APPLICATION FOR TODAY:

Whom will you follow: Jesus or the devil? Jesus makes the choice very clear.

80

JOHN 9

Jesus said: "*As long as I am in the world, I am the light of the world*" (John 9:5).

KEY MESSAGE:

JESUS IS THE LIGHT OF THE WORLD, AND LIGHT BRINGS TRUE VISION.

JOHN 9 CONSISTS OF one long narrative about Jesus bringing sight to a blind man and the various reactions to this miracle. There are many interesting aspects to this story, including the technique that Jesus used in this case. Often Jesus simply spoke a word of healing and the miracle occurred. In this case, however, Jesus put a clay mixture on the man's eyes and told him to go and wash it off in the pool of Siloam. When the man did this, he received his sight. I think the message here is that Jesus expects our faith to be active. The man could have said, "This is stupid" and simply brushed the clay off his face. But he didn't do that. Instead, he took action and received the miracle of healing.

A second important aspect of this narrative occurs in the discussion that takes place in verses one through five. Jesus' disciples assumed that the man's blindness was the result of someone's sin, either that of his parents or of the man himself. (It's hard to understand how they could think the man was to blame, given that he was born in this condition.) Today, many people fall into the same error: they think that bad things happen to bad people, so if you're suffering from some ailment, you must have sinned. Jesus makes it clear that this is not the case. He replies in John 9:3 that the blindness is not the result of anyone's sin, but rather it has given an opportunity for the "*works of God to be made manifest in him.*"

The first people to encounter the man after he receives his sight are his neighbours (vv. 8–12). They ask how he can now see, and he recounts the experience. When they ask him where Jesus is now, the man replies that he doesn't know. This makes sense: the man went to the pool of Siloam, and there's no indication that Jesus went with him. The neighbours then bring the man to the religious leaders, the Pharisees, to get their view of the matter. Always the religious sticklers, the Pharisees' immediate concern is that Jesus did this miracle—which would qualify as work—on the Sabbath Day. Therefore, the Pharisees conclude, Jesus cannot be from God. Others demur, however, asking how a sinner could perform such miracles. The Pharisees ask the healed man for his comments, and he describes Jesus as a prophet (v. 17). Some of the religious leaders aren't even prepared to acknowledge the possibility of the miracle until they check with the man's parents (vv. 18–24). They're able to confirm that this is their son, he was born blind, and he can now see. They aren't prepared to discuss the miracle for fear of excommunication from the synagogue (vv. 22–23).

John returns to a debate between the Pharisees and the healed man in verses twenty-four through thirty-four. This discussion ends in predictable fashion: the man avers that *"If this man were not of God, he could do nothing"* (v. 33), and the Pharisees respond by excommunicating him. But the man has a final encounter with Jesus, and one could say that Jesus and the man have the last laugh. In verses thirty-five through forty-one, Jesus reveals Himself to the man, who then believes in Him as Lord and worships Him (v. 38). Jesus directs His final message to the Pharisees: *"For judgment I am come into this world, that they which see not might see; and that they which see might be made blind"* (v. 39). The Pharisees perceive that these comments are directed at them and ask Jesus if He's calling them blind. Jesus replies: *"If you were blind, you would have no sin: but now ye say, We see; therefore your sin remains"* (v. 41).

APPLICATION FOR TODAY:

Refusing to admit your sin and to turn to Jesus simply leaves you in your sinful state.

81

JOHN 10

Then the Jews surrounded Him [Jesus] and said to Him, "How long do You keep us in doubt? If You are the Christ, tell us plainly." Jesus answered them, "I told you, and you do not believe. The works that I do in my Father's name, they bear witness of Me." (John 10:24–25, NKJV)

KEY MESSAGE:
JESUS IS THE GOOD SHEPHERD.

JOHN 10 CAN BE divided into two sections. In John 10:1–21, Jesus makes an extended analogy of Himself as the good shepherd and His followers as the sheep. In 10:22–42, Jesus has another discussion with the religious leaders of the day. The chapter ends at verse forty-two with an assessment that is almost identical to John 8:30 and John 11:45: *"And many believed on him there."*

The first section of the chapter contains many well-known descriptions of Jesus as the Good Shepherd, including these words: *"I am the good shepherd: the good shepherd giveth his life for the sheep"* (v. 11). The King James Version contains six uses of the word "shepherd" and fifteen of the word "sheep." In these verses, Jesus is very clear, even though He is speaking by way of analogy or parable: Jesus saves and protects His followers, and there is no other route to eternal life. In verses seventeen and eighteen, Jesus again makes reference to choosing to lay down His life for the sheep, and to take His life back up again—a further predictions of His eventual death and resurrection.

At the end of these comments, and just before His discussion with the religious leaders, we see the familiar division among the people. Some of them think Jesus is either mad or demon-possessed, while others ask how someone in that state could open the eyes of the blind.

The discussion between Jesus and the religious leaders is somewhat frustrating. Having asked Jesus to "tell us plainly" if He is the Christ, they then reject His answer. This is reminiscent of the times in the Old Testament when people asked various prophets for a clear word from God, only to reject it when they didn't like the message. Human nature doesn't change, and we are much the same today. How many times do we ask God for wisdom or an answer, only to turn away because the answer isn't the one we wanted to hear from Him?

In this passage, Jesus affirms that He is the Christ, again refers to God as His Father, and ends the response with the clear assertion that: *"I and my Father are one"* (v. 30). His message is so unmistakeable that the Jews respond by taking up stones, intending to stone Him to death. Jesus asks for which of the good works from His Father they intend to stone Him, and the Jews respond that it's not due to good works but for the alleged sin of blasphemy, by calling Himself God. Jesus immediately turns the table on them by quoting Psalm 82:6: *"I have said, Ye are gods; and all of you are children of the most High."* Given that the religious leaders knew the scriptures intimately, they likely also knew Psalm 82:2: *"How long will ye judge unjustly, and accept the persons of the wicked?"*

Jesus then offers them a clear choice: if they don't want to believe His words, they should assess His works. Are His deeds those of the Father or not? If His deeds are those of the Father, then they should believe in Jesus as His Son. Despite the fact that verse twenty-four says that the Jews "surrounded" Jesus, He again escapes out of their hands and goes beyond Jordan to the place where John the Baptist had originally been performing baptisms. This causes many to recall John the Baptist. They note that John did not perform any miracles, and that the words John said of Jesus are true (v. 41).

APPLICATION FOR TODAY:

Are you following the Good Shepherd in your daily walk?

82

JOHN 11

"Jesus said unto her, I am the resurrection, and the life: he that believeth in me, though he were dead, yet shall he live: And whosever liveth and believeth in me shall never die" (John 11:25–26a).

KEY MESSAGE:
JESUS IS THE RESURRECTION AND THE LIFE.

JOHN 11 FOLLOWS A familiar pattern: Jesus performs a miracle, and the religious leaders don't like it. In this case, however, the stakes increase. The miracle is raising Lazarus back to life after he had been dead for four days, and the reaction includes starting the plot to kill Jesus.

The story also shows us Jesus as the unique God-man who was always in control and knew what He was going to do next. In John 11:1–6, the sisters of Lazarus send word to Jesus that Lazarus is ill. Presumably, they hope and expect that Jesus will come and heal their brother. Instead, Jesus stays where He is for an additional two days. After this period of time, Jesus tells His disciples that they are going to head to Judea. He informs them that Lazarus has died and that He is going to go and *"awake him out of sleep"* (v. 11). Despite the fact that no one had come to give Him the news, Jesus knew that Lazarus was dead and that He was going to raise him back to life. Indeed, verse four implies that Jesus deliberately stayed in the area beyond Jordan until Lazarus had died so that God and Jesus would be glorified.

In 11:17–39, we're told that Lazarus had been in the grave for four days. His sister, Martha, somewhat morbidly (but accurately) is concerned about opening the grave because she notes that the body will have started to decompose and will (as the King James Version says, "*stinketh*"). Undeterred, Jesus has the stone rolled away. Based upon His words in verse forty-two, it appears as though Jesus had already been in communication with the Father and knew that Lazarus had been raised back to life. Jesus says that He knows that the Father always hears Him, but that He was speaking out loud so that those around might believe that God had sent Jesus into the world. He then cries with a loud voice and tells Lazarus to come forth out of the grave—and that is exactly what happens.

When news of this miracle reaches the Pharisees, they are not pleased. Even they concede that Jesus is doing many miracles (v. 47). It appears that the Pharisees, along with many of Jesus' disciples, wrongly believed that Jesus intended to establish an earthly kingdom and lead a rebellion against the Roman rulers. They certainly did not consider the possibility that the Romans might actually end up worshipping Jesus as Lord. As anyone who has been to the Vatican knows, that did in fact happen, although it didn't happen in the lifetime of these Pharisees. Their concern was that they could lose their own exalted positions and that the Jewish people would suffer and be crushed by the Roman rulers. We know that the Romans didn't tolerate rebellion. Caiaphas, the high priest, proposes the solution: let one man (Jesus) die for the people and save the rest of them. In verses fifty-one and fifty-two, John says that these words of Caiaphas were prophetic, even though the high priest didn't intend them that way. John says that Jesus would die for the Jewish nation "*And not for that nation only, but that also He should gather together in one the children of God that were scattered abroad*" (v. 52).

Knowing that the Jewish leaders intended to put Him to death, Jesus "*walked no more openly among the Jews*" (v. 54), for He knew exactly the time appointed by the Father for His death and resurrection, and it had to come in conjunction with the feast of the Passover. As that feast was near at hand, we are moving toward the climax of John's Gospel.

APPLICATION FOR TODAY:
Jesus is Lord over life and death.

83

JOHN 12

Jesus said: *"And I, if I be lifted up from the earth, will draw all me unto me"* (John 12:32).

KEY MESSAGE:
JESUS IS THE LIGHT OF THE WORLD.

THIS IS A CHAPTER of contrasts: light and darkness, sight and blindness, life and death, belief and unbelief, courage and fear. This is also the chapter where John describes Jesus' triumphal entry into Jerusalem, which we remember on Palm Sunday. However, John does so in just four verses (vv. 12–16) and in much less detail than the other three writers of the Gospels, particularly Matthew and Mark. Instead, John opens with an account of a feast with Mary, Martha, and Lazarus. John tells us that many came to the occasion, not just to see Jesus, but also to see Lazarus, whom Jesus had raised from the dead.

The contrasts between light and darkness come chiefly in the words spoken by Jesus. He urges the people to believe in and follow the light, that they might not walk in darkness. He says that He is the light of the world (v. 46) and that those who believe in Him will not walk in darkness. He assures the people that He hasn't come to judge the world but to save it, for the hour of judgment is coming. The contrasts between sight and unbelief flow from the contrast between light and darkness. John references the prophet Isaiah, who said that the people would have blind eyes and hardened hearts (Isaiah 6:9–10).

The contrast between life and death can be seen in the fact that Lazarus had been dead and then miraculously restored to life by Jesus. The topic is also addressed when Jesus refers to His impending death, burial, and resurrection. In John 12:24, Jesus says that unless a corn of wheat falls into the ground and dies, it will not bear any fruit. Our highlighted verse is an explicit reference to His crucifixion. Incidentally, this is one of the reasons why the song "Above All" (by Paul Baloche and Lenny LeBlanc) is theologically wrong. Jesus was *not* trampled on the ground but was lifted up to bring us life, even as Moses lifted up the bronze serpent in the Old Testament.

The contrast between belief and unbelief is seen in the many Jews who believed in Jesus (v. 11), while many *"believed not on him"* (v. 37). This is directly related to the contrast between courage and fear. In verse forty-two, John informs us that many of the chief rulers believed in Jesus but wouldn't confess Him in public for fear of being expelled from the synagogue by the Pharisees.

The chapter ends with a speech by Jesus, in which He again says that He has been sent to them by the Father and has not spoken His own words but those of the Father. He ends the chapter with a further offer of life everlasting.

APPLICATION FOR TODAY:

There is no middle ground. You either come to everlasting life through Jesus or everlasting death through unbelief.

84

JOHN 13

Jesus said: A new commandment I give to you, that you love one another; as I have loved you, that you also love one another. By this all will know that you are My disciples, if you have love for one another. (John 13:34–35, NKJV)

KEY MESSAGE:
LOVE ONE ANOTHER.

JOHN 13 PROVIDES AN account of the disciples' Passover meal with Jesus, which we have come to call the Last Supper. While this meal forms the basis for our observance of Holy Communion, we don't read much about that part of the evening in John's Gospel. Those events are described in detail by the other three Gospel writers. John chooses to summarize the Passover meal in one brief phrase: *"And supper being ended"* (v.2). John has other events to focus on.

As we know from his three epistles, John paid particular attention to Jesus' command to love one another. As a result, he here focuses on Jesus' sacrificial act of washing the feet of His disciples. Normally, this would be the responsibility of the lowest servant in a household. Feet were obviously dirty and unclean from walking about in those days. On this occasion, there was no servant present, and none of the disciples showed any inclination to take on this lowly task. It was thus a very poignant illustration when Jesus took on this role. It's also significant that even though He knew that Judas was going to betray Him, Jesus nonetheless included him among those whose feet He washed.

The other disciple whose actions are described is Peter. Peter was a very impulsive man. He stays true to form here, first protesting that he doesn't feel comfortable having Jesus wash his feet, and then, after hearing Jesus say *"If I do not wash you, you have no part with Me"* (v. 8, NKJV) replying, *"Lord, not my feet only, but also my hands and my head!"* (v. 9, NKJV). Notably, neither Peter nor any of the others offer to take Jesus' place and perform this act of servanthood.

Having completed the task, Jesus resumes His place and explains the lesson He has just taught them. Do not seek to be above others. Rather, be willing to sacrifice for them. Let everyone know that you are a disciple of Jesus by your acts of service. In some denominations, this act of foot-washing is still practised today. I've been part of this on a few occasions, and it was a very powerful spiritual experience for me. Both the act of washing someone else's feet and the act of receiving this blessing were extremely meaningful. On these occasions, the one doing the washing also told the recipient what it was that he or she appreciated about them. While it can feel rather awkward to be part of this ritual in our society today, I recommend it to you. On the occasions when I participated, it was as part of a retreat in conjunction with other spiritual activities, which helped set the tone for the event.

In speaking the words in the highlighted verses, Jesus summarized the teaching for the evening. Let others know that you are His follower by your love for all. This should still be the hallmark of Christianity. Not our strict adherence to doctrine—although that is important—but by our love.

APPLICATION FOR TODAY:
To whom can you show love today?

85

JOHN 14

Jesus said to him, "Have I been with you so long, and yet you have not known Me, Philip? He who has seen Me has seen the Father; so how can you say, 'Show us the Father'? Do you not believe that I am in the Father, and the Father in Me? The words that I speak to you I do not speak on My own authority; but the Father who dwells in Me does the works." (John 14:9–10, NKJV)

KEY MESSAGE:

THE FATHER, SON, AND HOLY SPIRIT ARE ONE AND WORK IN UNITY.

THIS CHAPTER IS AN extended discussion among Jesus and His disciples toward the end of the Last Supper. John records statements or questions from three of the disciples, along with Jesus' answers. During their discussion, Jesus also promises them that they will receive another Comforter in the person of the Holy Spirit (vv. 16–17, 26).

This passage is also known for Jesus' reply to Thomas: *"I am the way, the truth, and the life. No one comes to the Father except through Me"* (v. 6, NKJV). This is a very important verse today, when many want to assert that there are a variety of paths that lead to God. This is a popular belief, but it's simply not true. One can either accept what Jesus clearly says—that He is the one and only way to God—or one can reject it. But you can't profess to be a Christian and hold on to a vague notion that those of other faiths will somehow find a way into heaven.

The underlying theme of the chapter is the unity of the Holy Trinity—Father, Son, and Holy Spirit. In earlier chapters, Jesus often said that He and the Father are one. Now, on the eve of His arrest and eventual crucifixion, He introduces the promise of the Holy Spirit, the Comforter, who will arrive and *"teach you all things"* (v. 26). Jesus doesn't often use the word "the Son" to refer to Himself here. This is a very personal address, and the personal pronouns "I, me, and myself" are found throughout the chapter. They appear a total of sixty-eight times in thirty-one verses.

Jesus' words offer comfort to the disciples before the coming tumult; they also offer comfort to us in these turbulent days. First, we know that Jesus has gone to prepare a place for us and will welcome us with open arms (vv. 2–3). Secondly, Jesus assures us that we will do greater works than He has done because He has empowered His followers (vv. 12–14). It's sad that many Christians don't believe these words and seem to think that the age of miracles has passed, or at least that miracles and blessings are rare events that may or may not come today.

Thirdly, Jesus promises us that the Holy Spirit will teach us all things that we need to know. This teaching is later reflected in the epistle of James when he reminds us that if we lack wisdom, we simply need to ask God to supply it to us. Finally, in John 14:27, Jesus assures His followers that He is leaving us His peace and that we aren't to let our hearts be troubled or afraid. I take great comfort in the number of times God tells us not to be afraid. Clearly He understands that we have a tendency to be afraid when we face challenges, and it's good to remember that God is above any challenge we might face.

APPLICATION FOR TODAY:
Continue to trust God no matter what the circumstances might be.

86

JOHN 15

Jesus said: "*I am the vine, you are the branches. He who abides in Me, and I in him, bears much fruit; for without Me you can do nothing*" (John 15:5, NKJV).

KEY MESSAGE:
IT IS ESSENTIAL FOR US TO ABIDE IN JESUS.

THIS CHAPTER CONSISTS ENTIRELY of the words of Jesus. If you have an edition of the Bible that prints the words of Jesus in red, you'll notice that John 15 and 16 are almost entirely in red. The exceptions are small portions of chapter sixteen, when the disciples speak among themselves or respond to Jesus.

The words "abide" and "love" are repeated often in chapter fifteen. In the second half of the chapter, we also see use of the word "hate." The counterpart to love is that those who don't love Jesus will also hate His followers. We don't often use the word "abide" today. Webster's dictionary defines the word as to remain, stand fast, go on being. In short, we need to remain constantly in Jesus. He is the source of our strength.

In the first portion of this chapter, Jesus uses the analogy of a vine and its branches. If you cut a branch off a vine, it ceases to bear fruit. The same is true of us. When we abide in Jesus, we will continue to bring forth more fruit;

In the middle verses, Jesus again reminds His followers of the importance of loving one another. In verses twelve and seventeen, Jesus specifically tells His disciples to "*love one another.*" In verse thirteen, He underscores this command with a reference to His upcoming crucifixion: "*Greater love has no one than this, than to lay down one's life for his friends*" (NKJV).

Jesus then warns us that everything won't be rosy merely because we love Him and love others. In verse eighteen He pointedly says that the world will hate us because it hated Him first. Neither Jesus nor His followers are of the world, and the world doesn't like to be reminded of its sinful nature and actions. (Indeed, some gospel preachers today face backlash for using the word "sin." It's not always easy to proclaim the truth, but we are to abide in Jesus, not the world!) We need to call sin out for what it is. Even some popular Christian songs try to soft sell this point and minimize sin. One group altered a line from "Oh Little Town of Bethlehem." Instead of singing "cast out our sin and enter in," they replace "sin" with "fear." While God does cast out our fear, that's not the line in the original song, nor is it the key reason for the birth of Jesus.

To wrap up the chapter, Jesus again promises that the Holy Spirit will come to them, and that His disciples will *"bear witness, because you have been with me from the beginning"* (v. 27, NKJV).

APPLICATION FOR TODAY:
Abide in Jesus and show His love to the world.

87

JOHN 16

Jesus said: "These things I have spoken to you, that in Me you may have peace. In the world you will have tribulation; but be of good cheer, I have overcome the world."
(John 16:33, NKJV).

KEY MESSAGE:
JESUS OFFERS US TRUE PEACE IN ANY CIRCUMSTANCES.

THIS CHAPTER IS A continuation of Jesus' address to the disciples, which took place over the course of the evening of the Last Supper. Jesus' words in John 16, in particular, are much easier for us to understand today than they were for the disciples. We now have the completed Bible and know how the story ends. At that time, Jesus' words seemed so cryptic that John records the disciples asking what Jesus meant (vv. 17–18). The disciples' efforts to understand Jesus' words were further complicated by the fact that Jesus moved from one set of future events to another without providing further details. In this regard, His words remind me of the book of Isaiah, where the prophet moves from one time period to another without necessarily explaining that this is his method of speech.

Briefly, Jesus tells the disciples that (a) He is going away and they won't see Him; (b) He will come back again and they will see Him; (c) the Holy Spirit will come to them to instruct them and to convict the world of sin, righteousness, and judgment; and (d) there will be a period of time when each of them will be scattered and desert Jesus. We can readily see why their heads were spinning at the end of this address!

The underlying message is that Jesus provides joy and peace, which no one can steal from us, regardless of the circumstances: *"Therefore you now have sorrow; but I will see you again and your heart will rejoice, and your joy no one will take from you"* (v. 22, NKJV). These words should provide immense comfort to us, especially since we know that Jesus did triumph over the grave—something none of the disciples knew about when Jesus said these words to them.

APPLICATION FOR TODAY:
Jesus has already won the battle for us. We are victorious!

88

JOHN 17

[Jesus prayed to the Father] *"And this is eternal life, that they may know You, the only true God, and Jesus Christ whom You have sent"* (John 17:3, NKJV).

KEY MESSAGE:
JESUS PRAYED FERVENTLY FOR ALL OF HIS FOLLOWERS, INCLUDING US AND FUTURE GENERATIONS.

APART FROM THE OPENING words of John 17:1—*"Jesus spoke these words, lifted His eyes to heaven, and said"* (NKJV)—all of chapter seventeen consists of Jesus' great prayer for His disciples and followers, regardless of when they exist on this earth. Some commentators have said that this chapter is truly "the Lord's prayer," as it's Jesus' great prayer to His Father immediately before His arrest in John 18.

The prayer can be divided into three sections. The first section (vv. 1–5) consists of Jesus glorifying the Father and summarizing the work that He has completed on earth. These verses again remind us that there is only one true God, and that Jesus is His Son. They also remind us that Jesus offers us eternal life, as seen in the verse highlighted above.

In the second section (vv. 6–19), Jesus prays for His original disciples. He knows that they will face a very difficult task in continuing His work on earth after He returns to the Father. In verse fifteen, Jesus is clear that He's not asking the Father to remove His disciples from the world, but rather to keep them safe from the evil one. Jesus knows that His followers will suffer hatred and persecution for proclaiming God's message, which is at odds with how the world wants to live.

In the final section of the prayer (vv. 20–26), Jesus prays for all believers—including you and me. This is an awesome thought! Jesus says: *"Neither pray I for these alone, but for them also which shall believe on Me through their word"* (v. 20). One of Jesus' key requests in this prayer is for unity: *"That they all may be one"* (v. 21). In fact, the word "one" appears five times in this section of the prayer, and once more in verse eleven. In these verses we may find our own "great commission" just as surely as we see it in the final verses of Matthew 28. Jesus directs us to tell the world that God sent Him to the earth (v. 25) and that we show God's love to the world (v. 26).

Recently I read a book titled *Love Them Anyway* by Choco De Jesus.[7] It was a book I needed to read more than I wanted to read, because I know that I struggle to show God's love to those who are different from me or reject me. We need to remember that the world rejected Jesus too.

APPLICATION FOR TODAY:
When all else fails, love them anyway!

---

[7] Choco De Jesus, *Love Them Anyway* (Lake Mary, FL: Charisma House, 2021).

89

JOHN 18

"Jesus answered [Pilate], 'My kingdom is not of this world. If My kingdom were of this world, My servants would fight, so that I should not be delivered to the Jews; but now My kingdom is not from here'"
(John 18:36, NKJV).

KEY MESSAGE:
NOTHING CAN DERAIL OR ALTER GOD'S PERFECT PLANS.

THE KEY MESSAGE I'VE chosen for this chapter was brought to my mind again by a sermon I heard at Eastridge Baptist Church in Kent, Washington, on January 9, 2022. Pastor John Leprohon spoke about how God's plans cannot be thwarted. Even when secular, sinful people—including those in power—think that they act with autonomy, they may very well be fulfilling God's plan.

In this chapter, Jesus is arrested and brought to trial. God's plan to redeem all people required that Jesus' blood be shed to cleanse our sins. No plan of man would change that reality. John records that when Jesus said He was the man they were seeking, his arresters *"drew back and fell to the ground"* (John 18:6, NKJV). We're not told if this was an act of momentary remorse or fear, but it didn't stop them from their assignment. As Jesus says in other passages, He could have called legions of angels to come and defend Him, but that wasn't in accordance with God's plan.

As the arrest unfolds, two more remarkable events occur. First, Jesus says that the soldiers should allow His followers to leave, and they do so. This fulfills the prayer of Jesus in John 17:12. Secondly, Peter draws a sword and cuts off the right ear of the servant of the high priest. (Clearly, Peter was a better fisherman than swordsman!) One would naturally expect this to result in a corresponding attack by the soldiers, but it doesn't. God's plan was for Jesus to be arrested in a peaceful manner. In fact, Luke records that Jesus then proceeded to heal the servant before being led away (Luke 22:51). Luke also tells us that they had brought swords with them at Jesus' request, which fulfilled the words in Isaiah 53:12 that *"He was numbered with the transgressors"* (NKJV).

When Jesus is brought to trial, He doesn't offer any words to defend Himself. Before the high priest, He simply states that He hasn't said anything in secret, so if the leaders want to know what He taught, they only need to ask those who heard Him. We can recall, of course, that the religious leaders themselves heard much of Jesus' teaching, because they often debated with Him. Jesus' response results in one of the officers striking Him with the palm of his hand, but it doesn't provoke any anger in Jesus; He merely poses a question to the man.

Before Pilate, Jesus is courteous but not defensive. He answers Pilate's initial question ("Are you the King of the Jews?") with one of His own ("Are you speaking for yourself about this, or did others tell you this concerning Me?"). Jesus speaks the words shown in our highlighted verse, truthfully saying that He is a king but that His kingdom is not of this world. In answer to Pilate's further question, Jesus declares that He came into the world to bear witness to the truth, and that everyone who follows the truth will listen to Him. Pilate then responds, somewhat rhetorically, with the ironic question: "What is truth?" He had the living Truth standing directly in front of him and either didn't recognize it or didn't want to hear it!

The chapter concludes with Pilate declaring Jesus to be innocent and seeking to release Him, but the crowd calls out for the release of Barabbas. Pilate clearly had the authority to release Jesus, but that wouldn't have fulfilled God's plan. Even turning Jesus back to the religious court wouldn't suffice, because they didn't have the authority to put anyone to death.

You've probably heard that God has a plan for your life. Are you seeking to follow it? Many people say that they don't know God's will or plan for them. Often, they do have an inkling, but they're hoping that God will change His mind if they put Him on hold. This is a dangerous approach. God's plan will always be the best one for us. Take a moment to ask yourself if you know that you are following God. Did you do the last thing you know He told you to do? Sometimes we have fleeting moments of opportunity to be God's agent, and if we let the moment slip, it might not return. If you're in that position, seek God's forgiveness and ask Him to guide you as you move forward. It's never too late to begin again with God.

APPLICATION FOR TODAY:
Are you seeking to fulfil God's plan or are you struggling against it?

90

JOHN 19

"The Jews answered him [Pilate], 'We have a law, and according to our law He ought to die, because He made Himself the Son of God'" (John 19:7, NKJV).

KEY MESSAGE:
JESUS IS THE SON OF GOD.

I SELECTED VERSE SEVEN to highlight because it's another strong response to those who try to say that Jesus didn't declare Himself to be the Son of God. As we've seen in these devotions, Jesus most certainly did declare that He was the Son of God. Moreover, as this verse shows, those who heard Him speak and saw Him during His life clearly understood that to be His message. They didn't accept the message, for their hearts were hardened, but they certainly knew that Jesus declared Himself to be the Messiah.

In this chapter, Pilate tries to set Jesus free in verses six, twelve, and fifteen. Pilate eventually caves in to the pressure, because he fears the consequences for his own position if the Roman authorities agree with the crowd's assertion that allowing another king to live would be seen as hostility to Caesar. Whether he knew it or not, Jesus then died even for the sins of Pilate, including that of condemning a man he knew to be innocent. His act of defiance in labelling Jesus as *"the King of the Jews"* (v. 19) and refusing to change it to read "he said, I am King of the Jews" (as requested by the chief priests) doesn't exculpate him.

This chapter also provides several examples of how Jesus' death fulfilled Old Testament scriptures. These examples are important, because Jesus couldn't have manufactured any of them. When the soldiers cast lots for Jesus' clothing in John 19:23–24, they fulfill Psalm 22:18, both in dividing the garments and in casting lots for the coat. In verse thirty-six, the soldiers decide not to break Jesus' legs, because He's already dead, unlike the others who were crucified with Him. This fulfills Psalm 34:20. Finally, the fact that the soldiers looked at Jesus as He died was a fulfillment of Zechariah 12:10.

This chapter ends with two notable men obtaining the body of Jesus and placing it in a sepulchre. Joseph of Arimathea, who is referred to as a secret disciple of Jesus (due to his fear of the Jews), asks Pilate for permission to take the body. (Mark's Gospel refers to Joseph as *"an honourable counselor"* who also *"waited for the kingdom of God"* in 15:43.) Nicodemus, the Jewish leader who came to see Jesus in John 3 and spoke up for Him in John 7, provides the myrrh and aloes to anoint the body. The use of myrrh reminds us of the gifts presented to Jesus by the magi after His birth. While each of these gifts has its own verse in the carol "We Three Kings," I note than many artists are reluctant to include the verse about myrrh in their renditions. We need to remember that Jesus' death and resurrection are key elements in our faith. He was not merely a good teacher who lived and died a natural death.

APPLICATION FOR TODAY:

Jesus is the Messiah, the Son of God.

91

JOHN 20

"Jesus said to him, 'Thomas, because you have seen Me, you have believed. Blessed are those who have not seen and yet have believed'" (v. 29, NKJV).

KEY MESSAGE:
WE SERVE A RISEN SAVIOUR WHO OFFERS US PEACE AND THE GIFT OF THE HOLY SPIRIT.

THERE IS A POPULAR saying that "seeing is believing." As with many other things, our Christian faith turns this around and says that "believing is seeing." For example, after His resurrection, Jesus only appeared to those who had expressed their faith in Him during His life on earth. He did not, for example, show up to visit Pontius Pilate and say, "You were right. I am innocent. But don't worry. You can't keep a good man down."

We tend to look down on Thomas for his statement in John 20:25 that he wouldn't believe in the resurrection unless he could see the nail prints and put his hand into the hole in Jesus' side. Indeed, there is a popular expression about being a "doubting Thomas." In his defence, however, all Thomas was seeking was something that had already been provided to the other disciples: an actual appearance of the post-resurrection Christ. Earlier in the chapter, Peter, John, and Mary Magdalene went to the tomb, found it empty, and weren't sure what to make of this, but John says that *"he saw and believed"* (v. 8, NKJV). One must keep in mind that he is writing about himself in that verse. Mary Magdalene even mistook the risen Jesus for the gardener until Jesus called her by name. I think we need to be gracious to Thomas, and possibly admit that the words of Jesus in verse twenty-nine are to commend and reassure us and all who have believed in Him, even though we are yet to see Him face-to-face.

Jesus also reassures His disciples, including us, that He offers us His perfect peace. Three times in this chapter He says *"peace be unto you"* (vv. 19, 21, 26). It's noteworthy that this group of followers, who were so afraid of the Jews that they gathered behind closed doors, would shortly go on to change the world as they proclaimed the Christian message with boldness. Threats, prison, and even death couldn't stop them, because they had seen the risen Christ.

Jesus also promised His followers that they would receive the Holy Spirit (v. 21–22), and that He was sending them out, even as God the Father had sent Him. The message for us remains the same. As believers, we have the gift and the power of the Holy Spirit. We need not fear, for we have the peace of Christ. We are to go forth and change the world, not huddle behind closed doors in fear. There will be resistance and suffering along the way, but we need to remember that our message is eternal and that this world is not our final home.

APPLICATION FOR TODAY:

Peace be unto you.

92

JOHN 21

"Peter, seeing him [John], said to Jesus, 'But Lord, what about this man?' Jesus said to him, 'If I will that he remain till I come, what is that to you? You follow Me'" (John 21:21–22, NKJV).

KEY MESSAGE:
DO NOT CONCERN YOURSELF WITH WHAT OTHERS MIGHT DO; YOU FOLLOW JESUS.

THIS CHAPTER IS SOMETIMES referred to as "breakfast by the sea." It also marks a turning point in the lives of these disciples. It appears as though despite having seen the risen Christ, they weren't sure what to do next. Peter, who always seemed to be on the move, announced that he was going fishing. Apparently having nothing else to do, six additional disciples join him. John identifies five of the group by name: Peter, Thomas, Nathanael, James, and John (the latter two being referred to as "the sons of Zebedee," a term used for them quite often). John also mentions *"two others of His disciples"* (v. 2). It's possible that these unnamed followers weren't from the original group of twelve but rather from the larger group of followers, or that John either didn't recall their names or didn't consider them essential to the narrative.

In a scene reminiscent of their original call by Jesus, the men toil all night and catch nothing. Jesus then appears on the shore and opens the conversation by asking them if they had caught anything. After hearing their answer in the negative, He tells them to cast the net on the right side of their boat, which they do. They are rewarded with a significant catch: 153 fish.

It's interesting that the men follow Jesus' instructions to cast the net on the right side, even though they apparently don't recognize him at that time.

In the earlier incident (recorded in Luke 5), Simon Peter knew who Jesus was, and had just allowed his boat to be used as Jesus' teaching pulpit. In verse seven, John tells us that he was the first to recognize Jesus on this occasion. We're not told whether this was due to the catch of fish sparking his memory, or whether he finally realized who was speaking to them. Ever the impulsive one, Peter then plunges into the sea to reach Jesus, leaving the others to bring the boat to shore.

The scene that follows is the breakfast by the sea. Despite its short place in the narrative, I appreciate this scene as showing us that Jesus cares about our physical needs (the men had worked hard all night and were hungry) and wants to have fellowship with us. Whether one likes the phrase "*come and dine*" (KJV) or "*come and eat breakfast*" (NKJV), the thought of having a meal with Jesus and a few friends is delightful.

After the meal, Jesus turns to business. He restores Peter to true fellowship with Him and commissions him for the tasks to come. Just as Peter had denied Jesus three times, Jesus now gives him three opportunities to say that he loves Jesus. In each exchange, Jesus tells Peter to look after His followers, with the words "*Feed My lambs*" (v. 15, NKJV), "*Tend My sheep*" (v. 16), and "*Feed My sheep*" (v. 17). Jesus doesn't promise Peter an easy road. John notes that in verse eighteen, Jesus alludes to Peter's eventual martyrdom. Peter then asks the question set out in our highlighted verses. Jesus' response doesn't answer Peter's question, nor is it intended to. Rather, Jesus reminds Peter that his task is to follow Jesus and not be concerned with what the other disciples might do. That lesson is appropriate for us today.

In the balance of the New Testament, some disciples appear often and even author parts of the Bible, and there are others who are never mentioned again. Perhaps when we get to heaven, we'll be able to ask some of them what unfolded in their lives. Until then, it's up to each of us to follow Jesus and feed His flock.

APPLICATION FOR TODAY:

Follow Jesus and feed His sheep.

CONCLUSION

WHEN I STARTED WRITING this portion of the book, my original thought was to only discuss the "I am" statements of Jesus—those instances when He clearly told people that He was the Messiah. However, as I made my way through John's Gospel, each chapter came alive for me, and I saw some messages and insights I hadn't seen before. John ends his account by telling us that if someone wrote out everything Jesus did *"one by one, I suppose that even the world itself could not contain the books that would be written"* (John 21:25b, NKJV). There truly are endless insights into the heart of God within the pages of the Bible. I encourage you to spend time each day reading and absorbing God's Word. I don't know what God might call you to do, but I am confident that He has something for you to do as you follow Him. May the Lord bless you and keep you. Amen.

ABOUT THE AUTHOR

PHILIP EDWARD CARR WAS born and raised in Toronto, Ontario. He earned an Honours B.A. from York University in 1977, specializing in the study of English literature. His classes ranged from Chaucer and Shakespeare to a course in Canadian autobiography and autobiographical fiction. He went on to earn a Bachelor of Laws degree (LL.B.) from Osgoode Hall Law School at York University in 1980.

Philip moved to Calgary after graduation and had a long career in the legal profession. This included arguing one case in the Supreme Court of Canada. He retired from the legal profession at the end of 2018.

Philip has had many articles and letters published over the years. These include: "One Day Too Late" about his battle with depression (published in 2012 in *National*), "Help! I'm about to Become a Hockey Parent" (published in 2012 in *Calgary's Child*), and "Avoiding Vocational Hazards: Health and Wellness in Law" (published in 2019 in the *Christian Legal Journal*).

Philip is married to Linda Carr. They recently celebrated their forty-fourth wedding anniversary. They have three adult children and a spoiled cat named Marm. Philip and Linda are long-time members of Grace Baptist Church.

Volunteer service is very important to Philip. He has served as a board member for his church, as president of his local community association (twice), and as the provincial president for St. John Ambulance. He has also spoken and presented papers for Christian Legal Fellowship and the Canadian Bar Association.

You can write to Philip at this address: P.O. Box 65018, North Hill RPO, Calgary, AB T2N 4T6.